Singing with Your Whole Self

The Feldenkrais Method and Voice

Samuel H. Nelson
and Elizabeth Blades-Zeller

Illustrated by Amy Walts

The Scarecrow Press, Inc.
Lanham, Maryland, and London
2002

SCARECROW PRESS, INC.

Published in the United States of America
by Scarecrow Press, Inc.
4501 Forbes Boulevard, Suite 200
Lanham, Maryland 20706
www.scarecrowpress.com

4 Pleydell Gardens
Kent CT20 2DN, England

British Library Cataloguing in Publication Information Available

Library of Congress Cataloging-in-Publication Data

Nelson, Samuel H.
    Singing with your whole self : the Feldenkrais method and voice / Samuel H. Nelson
    and Elizabeth Blades-Zeller.
        p. cm.
    Includes bibliographical references and index.
    ISBN 0-8108-4049-9 (pbk. : alk. paper)
    1. Singing—Instruction and study.   2. Music—Performance—Physiological aspects. 3.
    Feldenkrais method.   I. Blades-Zeller, Elizabeth. II. Title.

MT821 .N45 2002
738'.04—dc21   200141093

Contents

Preface

Why This Book?

How does one develop an internal feel for what sounds good? How do you learn to use all of yourself when singing? What is the relationship between the felt sense (kinesthetic sense), effort, and good sound? These are the questions that led to this book. And curiously enough, they are questions that seem not to be addressed in books on the teaching of voice.

The voice pedagogical literature is replete with information on how the vocal mechanism works, what is the "correct" position for best vocal output, descriptions of the structures involved in making sound, and how to develop the vocal apparatus. The literature also contains numerous exercises to assist students of voice in the development and teaching of voice. But nowhere is there an in-depth exploration of developing kinesthetic sensitivity, what this does for sound, and how to bring all of oneself into use while singing. This book attempts to fill this gap.

The mechanism for developing kinesthetic sensitivity we will use is the Feldenkrais Method, an advanced sensory motor learning system. We will look at some of the key issues in developing the voice and see what insights can be gained from this unique perspective. We will then look at how we use ourselves and present lessons both to enhance our capacity to sing and to allow the vocalist to recognize and ameliorate temporary problems, be they illness or muscular strains, that crop up as one performs. For the latter there will be some "quick fixes."

Our intent, therefore, is to provide both intellectual and experiential knowledge that will allow the vocalist to reach and perform at his or her peak much of the time.

What Is This Book?

This book is a handbook, not a scholarly tome. It is intended for use. It is not a scientific treatise or a report on quantified scientific research, but we feel that it embodies the important scientific work by the creator of the Feldenkrais Method, Moshe Feldenkrais, D.Sc. Trained at the Sorbonne, Feldenkrais was a physicist and electrical engineer who for many years in the 1930s was an important collaborator of Nobel Prize–winner Pierre Joliet-Curie. His creation of the Feldenkrais Method involved the application of the important scientific principles of predictability and replication to human movement. Feldenkrais, as a good physicist, worked from first principles in creating this method. Much of his work is simple applications of mechanics to human functioning at the most basic levels. Thus, for example, he would note the small counterweights that made for effective movement.

We have attempted to give the reader/doer a feel for this approach in the text. On many occasions a claim will be made that can be easily verified by performing the movement experiment that follows it. On other occasions the experiment involved is a thought experiment. Dr. Nelson has a master's degree in economics and worked for half a decade at Argonne National Laboratory, where most of his colleagues were Ph.D.'s in physics. He is thus intimately familiar with this type of experiment.

Acknowledgments

We would like to thank the following:

Amy Walts, our illustrator, who rose from her sickbed to finish preparing the illustrations for this book.

Wendy Burwell, whose editorial advice was greatly appreciated if not always followed.

Cindy Dietrich-Bloomberg and Steve Bloomberg, whose help in preparing the final version of this book for the printer was invaluable.

Matthew Zeller, who scanned diagrams for us.

The Heidelberg College Choir, who took the modular lessons on tour and found them helpful.

The cast of *Annie Warbucks* at Midlakes High School in Phelps, New York, who liked the lessons so much they insisted that Dr. Nelson do a short lesson in standing as the warm-up opening night.

And the many students who have used the written lessons contained in this book and whose success convinced us of the validity of this concept.

1

Overview

RELATING THE FELDENKRAIS METHOD TO THE TEACHING OF SINGING

The intention of every committed voice teacher is to guide the student to find the freest, most beautiful sound and to develop that voice until it becomes consistently accessible and expressive. Along the path of this journey, the teacher may seek to guide the student to associate certain sensations with that free, beautiful sound. Yet, while some students may already have a well-developed kinesthetic awareness that makes instant connection to these sensations, many more do not. Even that more highly kinesthetic student can often have subtle barriers that prevent ease and freedom. An empathic teacher may sense these blocks and know that the student is locking up, may be able to see tension in the shoulders or, through resulting sound, hear tension in the tongue. The standard approach to address such tension is to direct the student to perform some limbering-up movement, such as shoulder rolls, or to try consciously to fix the problem with a "manual" solution. But the body's neurology may not respond to such conscious, analytical commands to change. One has to speak to the body in its own neurological language, much as computers understand "machine language," which is in binary computer code. The Feldenkrais Method uses the body's neurological language to break down those subtle barriers, resulting in an almost magical adjustment that truly frees the singer and the voice.

As a team made up of a voice teacher and an accomplished Feldenkrais practitioner, we have witnessed a number of these magical moments. The following two accounts are from individual joint lessons. Dr. Nelson did hands-on work (Functional Integration; see appendix for details) after he and Dr. Blades-Zeller had identified physical problems while a student sang. Dr. Blades-Zeller

1

has seen similar, though perhaps less dramatic, results in her studio with the modules from the lessons in this book.

Kevin

Kevin was a nineteen-year-old college vocal performance major. He was tall (six feet three inches [190 cm] and growing) and very lean and had a taut, well-muscled abdomen; hence, his range and vocal stamina were impeded. His inhalation was restricted, owing in part to an overly muscled torso coupled with a slight misunderstanding of rib expansion (he was not opening around the full circumference). Dr. Nelson stood beside him and gently worked with the ribs in relation to breathing on one side until Dr. Nelson felt the breathing open. Then he did the same thing on the other side. This took about ten minutes. Then Kevin sang. His voice was much fuller and the range was wider. And he was also breathing better in back.

Situations such as this, where a student "does" what he hears a teacher suggest but has actually misunderstood the suggestion, are quite common. Often, as in this case, the student will strain another part of the body to "do" what is asked without even realizing it. At other times the student's interpretation of the request will differ from what the teacher is really asking—for example, trying to move from the tailor's hips (actually the pelvic crest) when asked to move the hip.

Donna

Donna, who is quite short, is an alto. She works as a computer programmer. Before the joint session with Dr. Nelson and Dr. Blades-Zeller, she had been seeing Dr. Nelson for Functional Integration for about a year. During that time, she had learned to let go of the habitual generalized tension that had prompted her to begin the lessons and had also been in an automobile accident. Fortunately, thanks to the seat belt and air bag, she was only shaken up and slightly bruised. However, the accident, as any significant trauma would, had caused her to revert somewhat to her former state. It took three lessons over two weeks for her to recover from this incident.

When her joint lesson began, Donna was holding a great deal of tension in her neck and shoulders. She also tended to push her head forward, which tends to cloud the voice. Also, her voice was already somewhat husky and a little thin. Dr. Nelson did a short standing lesson to lengthen the neck and release the shoulders. After a few minutes, when the neck released, he stopped. Donna felt taller and looked straighter. When she sang, her voice was much clearer and more free. The clouded sound was gone, and her voice was full bodied.

OVERVIEW OF THE FELDENKRAIS METHOD

The Feldenkrais Method is a self-discovery process using movement. Its aim is to produce an individual organized to perform with minimum effort and maximum efficiency. Efficient organization is developed using the "organic" learning style of our early childhood, the way we learned to hold up our head, crawl, and so on. As such, it is an open-ended developmental learning process, which, like making music, offers infinite possibilities for refinement. The movements used are simple, gentle, pleasant, exploratory, and fun. They are usually repeated a number of times to clarify and enhance performance. The focus is always on the how-to of the movement, not the how much, how fast, or how hard. The movement always starts where the person is now. People are asked only to perform what they can do comfortably. They are actively discouraged from moving outside their comfort range.

The Feldenkrais Method has two aspects: Awareness Through Movement (ATM), a guided group movement lesson; and Functional Integration (FI), a hands-on session with a practitioner. The two are interrelated so that many lessons may be transposed from one to the other, much as a piece of music can be transposed from violin to piano. The work we will be presenting will, for obvious reasons, consist of only ATM. For a short explanation of FI, see the appendix.

In applying the Feldenkrais Method, individuals are led through movement sequences designed to introduce or clarify a function (e.g., sitting, breathing, reaching forward, or a more complicated function). They are thus led to "discover" a better way to perform this function, a way that involves more of themselves than their habitual way. Because, for the most part, this discovery involves the part of the nervous system that controls movement, as opposed to conceptual consciousness or "thinking," changes tend to be retained and often amplified. Typically, the changes in functional capacity are accompanied by greater pleasure in movement and often (for adults) an enhanced joie de vivre.

Our inefficient movement patterns are a result of our humanness. For unlike animals, such as dogs and horses, we are born knowing virtually nothing about movement. Thus, while it takes a foal perhaps five minutes after birth to get up and move around, it takes a normal human child about half a year to start crawling. Instead of inborn knowledge, we have an enormously powerful brain that is highly adept at learning. So as infants we learn how to sit, stand, roll over, walk. Some of this learning is done by trial and error and some by imitation. Because our learning is spotty, we learn some movements well, others poorly, and some not at all; over time, problems arise. We develop aches and pains or find ourselves unnecessarily restricted. In addition, injuries can cause problems both immediately and years later. Some individuals have problems that are caused by structural difficulties, for example, curvature of the spine (scoliosis).

The Feldenkrais Method, by helping to reprogram the functioning of our nervous system, facilitates our overcoming many of the problems arising from faulty initial learning, injuries, and structural problems.

The Feldenkrais Method is named after its originator, Moshe Feldenkrais, D.Sc. Feldenkrais developed the method to prevent being wheelchair bound by knee problems. In his twenties he severely injured one knee playing soccer. While hobbling around with this "bad" knee, he injured the other one. Eventually, the knee problems disappeared, and he went to the Sorbonne to study physics and electrical engineering. While there, he earned his doctorate, worked with Dr. P. Joliot-Curie, and met Dr. J. Kano, the founder of judo. This meeting spurred him to a serious study of judo, which led him to be the first European to earn a black belt.

When his knee problems resurfaced in the 1940s and threatened his walking, he asked the surgeons two questions: What are the odds of success? What does failure mean? He was told that the expectation of success was 50 percent and that failure could mean a wheelchair. He then determined that delay would not change the odds of a successful operation and decided to see what he could do for himself. Thus began a painstaking investigation of how he organized himself to move. In this investigation he used his knowledge of movement from judo, mechanics from physics, and what he proceeded to learn of anatomy, kinesiology, and physiology. A key question in this process was, If I take one hundred steps and on only one does my knee give out, what did I do differently that one time? The result of this investigation, beyond recovery of walking, was minute attention to the details of function—how one sits, stands, bends to the side, rotates. It was this attention to function that led Feldenkrais to originate his method.

KEY IDEAS IN THE DEVELOPMENT OF THE FELDENKRAIS METHOD

There are five key ideas involved in the development of the Feldenkrais Method: (1) life as a process, (2) involvement of the whole self as necessary for effective movement, (3) learning as the key activity of humans, (4) the necessity of choice, and (5) the logic of human development. That life is a process should be self-evident. No one is truly the same person he was ten years ago, nor will he be the same next year as he is now. This time period can be very short and the statement will remain true. As we approach a day, an hour, a minute, the difference becomes so small as to be nonexistent for practical purposes. In a similar vein, each time a piece of music is approached, it seems a little different, as one perceives different aspects of the same piece. The dynamics of process embedded in the Feldenkrais Method are much the same as this musical experience. The names of the two components reveal this: Awareness Through Movement illustrates that it is the awareness of what we are doing that is intended, and in Functional Integration the intent is to integrate our being around a function—sitting, breathing, reaching—in such a way that performance of that function (and related functioning) is altered. This process orientation means that, although it may be helpful to know about the structure or the static situation of the individual, it is not necessary for successful work with the Feldenkrais Method.

Any action, to be completely efficient and effective, must involve the whole self. That is, all parts of the organism must support and enhance the act. When this is not the case, some areas either are not involved or are acting counter to the intended act, or both. This invariably leads to a greater energy requirement to perform any action than when all of oneself is involved, for if any areas are not involved, some effort must be expended to prevent their moving, whether the person is aware of this or not. For example, bend your wrist downward. Did you notice that you curved your fingers? Now keep the fingers straight as you bend your wrist. Can you feel the difference? If not, try both again, slowly. Did you feel how much more effort is required when the fingers do not participate? The excess energy required either is dissipated as heat from excess friction or results in excessive muscular tension (friction per se is necessary to life, for without it walking, among other things, is impossible). It is the wear and tear of this excess friction and muscular tension that causes so many movement-related problems, such as backaches, carpal tunnel syndrome, and many arthritic conditions. Finding ways to approximate more closely the ideal of using the entire self in each act underlies the Feldenkrais work.

Of all living creatures on Earth, human beings are the furthest from adult functioning at birth. Accordingly, they must learn more than any other animal. Indeed, for the first few years of life we are insatiable learners. Nor does learning stop at adulthood. Rather, it goes on throughout life as we adjust to external and internal changes.

> In short, we may say that the human brain is such as to make learning, or acquisition of new responses, a normal and suitable activity. It is as if it were capable of functioning with any possible combination of nervous interconnections until individual experience forms the one that will be preferred and active. The actual pattern of doing is, therefore, essentially personal and fortuitous. . . .
>
> This great ability to form individual nervous paths and muscular patterns makes it possible for a faulty functioning to be learned. The earlier the fault occurs, the more ingrained it appears, and is. Faulty behavior will appear in the executive motor mechanisms which will seem later, when the nervous system has grown fitted to the undesirable motility, to be inherent in the person and unalterable. It will remain largely so unless the nervous paths producing the undesirable pattern of motility are undone and reshuffled into a better configuration. (Feldenkrais 1949, 40)

What Feldenkrais developed was a superior way to use movement to perform this reshuffling, a way that can help anyone function better. Indeed, Feldenkrais believed that our movement was sufficiently imperfect that a person with "no problems" could use an FI for each year of age and could benefit from ATM ad infinitum. Humans are particularly constituted so that learning is possible and pleasurable throughout their lifetime.

A person who has no choices in actions is considered compulsive. This is not a desirable state. Feldenkrais believed that it was not a fully human state. If there are only two choices, the situation is not much different. We advance to being mechanical, always choosing either A or B. All of us exhibit some movement and learning areas in which we are either compulsive or mechanical. They are generally not important to us, either because the matter is itself minor or because we structure our life so that it is minor. Dr. Nelson, for example, knows only one way to knot a tie. So either he wears a tie and ties it that way, or he does not wear a tie. It is a mechanical decision. If he had a bow tie or a bolo, he would have a third option and could truly exercise choice. Although having even more options is desirable, it is the creation of the third option that makes effective choice possible. It is at this point that the organism ceases to be locked into responding compulsively or mechanically and becomes alive and human. It is, therefore, the intent of Feldenkrais practitioners to help their students create options for themselves. This is done by presenting alternatives during each lesson that allow the nervous system to choose better ways to accomplish a function.

In helping a person increase functionality, it is important to follow the logic of human development. You cannot expect someone to run who cannot walk. For example, consider the brain of a damaged child. The first step is to ascertain where she is in her development, then what would normally come next, and finally find a means to evoke this normal development. The same type of thinking is used in other problems, only the question now becomes either, What is the logical development to reestablish effective action? or, What seemingly unrelated problem is involved? *The Case of Nora: Body Awareness as Healing Therapy* relates Feldenkrais's use of this style of thinking to help a woman recover from the damage caused by a brain hemorrhage. Although she was able to walk and hold an intelligent conversation, she had lost the ability to read and write and had difficulty locating doors, often walking into them. After several years, she was brought to Feldenkrais as a last hope before placement in a nursing home. He found that she had no concept of left and right. Therefore, he proceeded to help her reestablish her frame of reference. With considerable difficulty, they reestablished her frame of reference while she was lying on her back. When she had learned left and right on her back, she was turned over. In this position she had to learn it all over again. In other words, these concepts were not internalized but were related to external objects such as the couch. It took about two months to internalize her frame of reference completely.

An essential ingredient of human development used with Nora was reducing tension, thereby increasing sensitivity and allowing the organism to sense and respond to small changes. This stimulates our childlike learning capacity. Because children's attention is directed by curiosity, they do not exercise like adults but rather repeat a movement for the sheer pleasure of it. Moving in this way is free of tension and maximizes the potential for growth and learning. Also, because children are much weaker than adults, they are incapable of tensing their muscles as powerfully. As sensitivity decreases with effort, this automatically makes them more sensitive than adults. Thus, by attracting our curiosity once more to movement and reducing tonus (muscle tone), we evoke again the child's style of learning.

These then are the principal ideas that underlie the efficacy of the Feldenkrais Method.

KINESTHETIC IMAGINATION

> What you can do you can imagine, and what you can imagine you can do.
>
> —M. Feldenkrais

How good is your self-image? Not in the usual sense of how well do you think of yourself, but, rather, can you *sense* yourself? That is, how accurately can you sense yourself both statically and in movement? For example, if you think of your hands, do you represent them equally well, or do you have a greater sense of your dominant hand? Now lean forward. How much of yourself did you feel was involved in this movement? You probably felt the involvement of your back muscles. But did you also sense the shift in the thigh muscles? What about your buttocks? In truth, none of us accurately represents ourselves to ourselves at all times. Most people do not even attempt this. It is this representation of ourselves that is known as the kinesthetic image (or felt sense).

Developing a more accurate kinesthetic image is immensely valuable because it allows you to know more completely what you are doing. Otherwise, you may inadvertently introduce tension into your system. It also allows you to notice excess tension *before* it becomes a major problem. Any tension beyond the minimum necessary is both wasteful and harmful. Fortunately, humans have repair mechanisms, since no one can operate perfectly efficiently. Of necessity, living involves some damage and repair. Unfortunately, these repair mechanisms diminish with age. What one can get by with as a youth becomes problematical in middle age and can be painful as an old person. Hence, a well-developed kinesthetic image can make one more comfortable and effective. Finally, one can make performance-enhancing changes by using kinesthetic imagination to develop a more accurate kinesthetic image. Many musicians injure themselves needlessly because they cannot feel what they are doing until too late and because they practice for too long. Overlong practice usually involves excessive tension if there is a difficulty with a piece. The usual approach is to keep practicing, even though this may be frustrating. In this situation one becomes fatigued, which is when most injuries occur. By using kinesthetic imagination, it is possible both to shorten the learning time and to find ways to achieve the desired sound, dramatically reducing the likelihood of injury.

Practice makes perfect. However, if you practice something incorrectly, you perfect your errors. This is why it is so very difficult to change one's way of singing and performing. Indeed, the internal image for "correct" performance becomes this wrong way of doing. It is this difficulty that often results in failure to get it right in spite of hours of practice. Kinesthetic imagination is the ideal tool for this situation. It allows you to change the internal image that is the basis of the problem. In short, if you can change the internal program, the performance problem disappears, almost like magic.

Dr. Nelson worked extensively with a young violinist at the Eastman School of Music. One time she came in unable to complete a passage in a piece she was learning without running out of bow. She picked up her bow and played the piece and, as usual, ran out of bow during the passage. He asked her just to imagine playing the piece kinesthetically. When she came to the difficulty, she broke into a big smile. Even without the instrument, she had run out of bow! So the problem was clearly in her internal organization of the section. She was asked to imagine playing the section with the bow being long enough. After she could do this three times, Dr. Nelson asked her to pick up her violin and play. This time there was plenty of bow. Now when she practiced the piece, she could perfect it instead of perfecting her error.

Helping you develop your kinesthetic imagination is one of the major objectives of this book. It follows naturally from doing the lessons, for they increase your kinesthetic awareness. But it is a skill that must be developed. Accordingly, some lessons call for you to imagine a movement and then to do it. You may also use this practice when doing any lesson or activity. Slowly and gently do a simple movement, such as opening your mouth or lifting your foot. Choose a movement you are comfortable with. Notice how you do this movement as you do it. Now imagine the same movement. Then do the movement again. Notice how completely you represented this movement in your imagination. Then imagine it a few more times including something you missed the last time you imagined it. Alternate between imagining and doing it several more times. The last time you imagine, you will find that there is far more to the movement than what you first imagined. You will also notice that you cannot imagine a movement without actually doing it (at a reduced level). For example, imagine moving your right shoulder forward. Can you feel the subtle movement forward of the shoulder muscles? A close observer would actually see this very slight movement. Because our imagination and actuation (kinesthetically) are fundamentally the same, this approach allows us to bypass obstacles that we did not realize we had put in our own way.

A final advantage for musicians of kinesthetic imagination is the ability to practice noiselessly. There are many times when you otherwise cannot practice: when you are with someone who is asleep, when no practice room is available, and when you are on a public conveyance. In these situations and many others, unless you learn to practice noiselessly, you will not be able to practice.

RELATIONSHIP OF THIS WORK TO PEDAGOGICAL LITERATURE

> The position of the Body must be erect, the Shoulders thrown back, with the arms crossed behind, this will open the chest and bring out the Voice with ease.
> —Manuel Garcia (father), *Exercises and Method for Singing,*
> rule 4, 1819–22

> Good Posture: Chest comfortably high, spine and neck straight with head level; weight slightly forward on the toes with one foot somewhat in advance of the other . . . the toes should turn out slightly.
> —Van Christy, *Expressive Singing,* 1967

> Correct body alignment begins with the placement of the singer's weight forward on the balls of the feet, heels on the floor, feet being best placed slightly askew, one somewhat in front of the other depending upon the singer's height and weight. The tailbone is tucked or rolled under, causing the pelvis to shift forward.
> —Larra Browning Henderson, *How to Train Singers,* 1979

> The generally accepted stance for a good singing posture is as follows: The feet should be planted firmly on the floor, slightly apart (approximately 12 inches, 300mm), one slightly ahead of the other. The weight should be on the forward portion of the feet, to allow greater flexibility in breathing and also to create a more energetic impression.
> —Jan Schmidt, *Basics of Singing,* 1998

The Arched Palate: an imaginary soprano . . . looks into her throat by means of a mirror to see what is happening. At the same time that she sees her tongue lower itself at the back, with a groove forming from root to blade, she will probably also see an arching of the velum, or soft palate.

—William Vennard, *Singing: The Mechanism and the Technique,* 1967

When the larynx is low and the velum is high, the pharynx is somewhat longer vertically than horizontally. I draw the student's attention to this vertical feeling and ask for a "more vertical sound" when the sound becomes shallow or loses resonance. Once I heard Marilyn Horne explain that the vertical feeling had a great deal to do with her own singing. She said that she sings as if a pencil were standing in her throat with the eraser on her larynx and a sharp lead pointed toward her soft palate. "If that doesn't keep the palate high, nothing will!"

—Richard Alderson, *Complete Handbook of Voice Training,* 1979

For years, conscientious voice teachers have attempted to describe the myriad facets of free vocal production with clearly described instructions. Unfortunately, what may have begun merely as an astute observation of a natural, unconscious occurrence has acquired the irrefutable status of "vocal gospel." We can understand how this might have happened:

1. Astute voice teacher (such as Garcia II, Marchesi, Vennard) closely observes outstanding natural singer in action.

2. Astute teacher notes vocal production, reports it through written description—for example, "When A sings, the back wall of the pharynx is large and wide, with the velum (soft palate) high, resulting in a rich, full tone."

3. Reader of report thinks, "Aha! In order to have a rich, full sound, I have to be sure that my soft palate is high."

4. Reader instructs student, "Lift your soft palate!" Student dutifully attempts to raise the back wall of the pharynx through conscious muscular effort. Tension (inadvertently) results.

5. Description becomes gospel, unquestioned, imposed, *but not felt.* Passed on from generation to generation, the misunderstanding is perpetuated.

This phenomenon occurs in other performance disciplines. For instance, the fledgling equestrian is told to "keep your heels down." This is because riders have a tendency to push their toes down, which makes it possible for the toe of the boot to accidentally push through the stirrup. This could lead to the rider being dragged in the event of a fall. Heeding this admonishment, the rider tends to push the heel down forcefully and far, considerably below the toe. This distorts the posture, creating tension in the ankles, leg, and back. (If you raise your feet from the floor while sitting and push your heels down hard, you can feel this for yourself.) It's not nice for horses either. Dr. Nelson once saw a woman who rode like this bring an obviously lame horse to a workshop with Linda Tellington-Jones. Linda, a certified Feldenkrais practitioner, applied the Feldenkrais Method to horses to create TTEAM (a method of working with horses to improve the horses' functionality). When she mounted the horse, she rode with her feet basically level; if you took away the horse, it would be like sitting in a chair. The horse's lameness disappeared while she rode. The horse was, indeed, slightly lame, but most of its lameness was due to the way the rider rode.

It is our incredible intelligence and adaptiveness, combined with the inability of words to completely map actions, that lead to this situation. You tell someone something, and they do what they think they've been told. Because we are very adaptive, we do it even if it feels wrong. Over time it becomes the way we do it, or "normal." And what is normal feels right to us even when it isn't. This way of doing something then gets passed on and becomes accepted truth.

However, it appears that the field of vocal pedagogy is at last moving into a new era of body-mind awareness. Today's voice teachers must now take responsibility for developing their own kinesthetic awareness in order to guide their students effectively. It is no longer suitable merely to say, "Do this, do that. Lift the soft palate! . . . Keep the tongue forward. . . . Sing from the diaphragm! . . . Keep your chest high!" We must enable students to tune into their own kinesthetic sensibilities and find the natural coordination that in time becomes spontaneous—by working with the body in its wisdom rather than through manipulation. This cannot happen unless the teacher also comes to understand natural body function, becoming kinesthetically aware in order to feel undue interference and tension. A teacher who actually experiences such tension will never again resort to the use of a vocal myth without considering the negative effects.

With this book we hope to redress many misconceptions and much misinformation that, through repetition without inquiry, have perpetuated a number of the vocal myths that have become gospel to the teaching of singing.

Awareness Through Movement

Awareness Through Movement is usually done in a group. In ATM students are verbally guided through movement sequences designed to clarify a function, such as side-bending or turning. This allows a superior form of functioning to be adopted. Emphasis is on the learning process, the "how" of doing. Movements are typically gentle and slow. Sensitivity to what you do is most important. According to Weber-Fechner's law, the ability to detect a change in a stimulus varies inversely with the intensity of the stimulus (see Shafarman 1997, 179–80). Put more simply, effort and sensitivity are inversely related. Therefore to maximize sensitivity, one must reduce effort. Movements are intended to be within the individual's comfort range; the production of pain or discomfort is avoided, as it is a bar to learning and increased awareness. Students are often asked to notice what they do and how they do it throughout their entire self. For example, what does the lower spine do when the head is lifted? Because learning is a highly individual matter, ATM is not competitive. Students are encouraged to proceed and learn at their own pace.

Because of the central role sensitivity plays in learning about oneself, in a typical ATM class most lessons are done lying on the floor. Since sensitivity is inversely related to effort, the least effortful position to perform a particular lesson is usually the best for learning. Because of the special needs of choirs (and other musicians), we have created a series of full-length lessons most of which can be performed in chairs. Working through them will increase your kinesthetic image and provide a sense of ease and grace. The lessons have been modularized so that they may also be used as warm-ups.

Introduction to the Lessons

The lessons have been divided into short, seven- to ten-minute modules. If you have the time to do the lesson in one sitting, that is preferable. The effects are more noticeable and more lasting. However, in today's hectic life, that is not always possible. Modularizing the lesson makes it possible to gain almost as much benefit, only spread out over more time. This is particularly true if you work through one lesson at a time and can do at least one module a day until you really have the feel of the entire lesson. Another advantage of the modules is that they are an appropriate length for warm-ups. Because choirs and choruses usually lack comfortable floor space for all members to lie down, these lessons were designed wherever possible to be done in chairs.

The lessons can be performed with only modest preparations. Unless otherwise specified, please take off your shoes, if possible, before beginning the lesson. Also, make sure you have a reasonably comfortable chair to sit in, that is, a chair where your feet reach the floor with your knees bent. If you are quite short, get a book or two to place beneath your feet. If you are over six feet tall, most chairs are too short. Therefore, sit on a cushion or some books so that the chair is comfortable. *Whenever possible, modify your environment to suit yourself.* Try to avoid forcing yourself to conform to an uncomfortable situation. However, be clear that comfort is also a function of habit, and if your habitual way of being is injurious, some temporary discomfort may be desirable. For example, many teenagers slouch when they sit. This posture will eventually cause trouble, and, of course, even with the young and supple, it impairs the ability to sing. However, until one learns to sit upright comfortably—that is, with the spine carrying the weight—the upright position is often forced and, therefore, uncomfortable. Just ask anyone whose mother told them to "Sit up straight" how comfortable a forced upright position is!

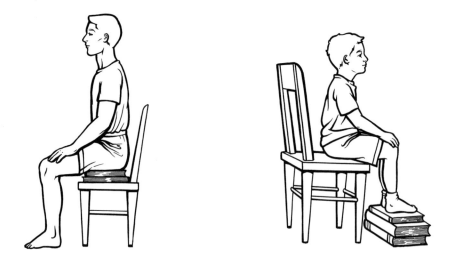

All the movements in the lessons should be done slowly and attentively. Take as long between separate movements as it takes to do the movement. If there is any pain, stop *immediately*. If you grow fatigued, *stop*. In both these cases you can kinesthetically imagine doing the movement. That is, imagine what it feels like to do the movement. For example, imagine making a fist. Did you *feel* the contractions of the muscles? Try it a few more times to get clearer about *feeling what it is you are imagining*. We shall go further with this concept in a later chapter.

Please remember that *how you do what you do* is what is of value in this play/work. Thus, two or three repetitions done with attention, where the system has the chance to observe what it is doing and learn, are far more valuable then ten or twenty or more movements done mechanically. Also, the movements should, in some sense, be *enjoyable.* If they are done as a chore or to accomplish some external goal, they become vastly less effective. This is especially true if you override feelings of pain or discomfort. In such a case, the continued movements can be *harmful.* Thus, allowing yourself the time to make the movements pleasant is crucial. If you are short on time, do fewer repetitions and do them slowly. Do not try to make the movements faster.

It is very common to feel that you are not doing a lesson correctly. If this is the case, *do not panic.* Instead, reread the directions, then repeat the lesson as you now understand it. If you still feel that what you are doing is not correct, there are two possibilities.

First, you could be wrong, and what you are doing is a correct interpretation of the instructions. However, if it feels wrong to you because it currently is very difficult or impossible, don't worry. Learning sometimes entails doing that which is difficult. During a Feldenkrais training program every participant will experience this difficulty or feeling of impossibility more than once. However, when you persist, magical things happen. Sometimes you suddenly find yourself able to do the movement. Or the next day, or the next time you do the lesson, you may discover that the impossible has become doable, and the doable pleasant.

Second, you could be right. You could be doing the wrong movement. However, if you do this movement in a careful attentive way that avoids pain and discomfort, the worst that can happen is nothing. In all likelihood, you will learn something about your movement. And quite possibly the next time you try the lesson, the "right" movement will come to you.

Also, please realize there is no absolute right way. Each person is different. Therefore, we must each discover our own present best way. These lessons will enable you to do that. Further, please realize that the "worse" you are at the start, the more benefit you will get from a lesson. Thus, do not focus on some-one else's "accomplishment" or skill, but on improving your own kinesthetic awareness and abilities.

You should, when possible, repeat a movement many times until you feel it to be easy (or at least easy by comparison with your first attempt). Often twenty repetitions are useful. Take the suggested number of repetitions in these lessons as minimums. If you feel the value of doing more, by all means do so. Each time you repeat a movement, notice what is different as you refine it. Do not worry about doing the movement badly. Doing badly is merely a part of learning. If we only acted when we did things well, we would do very little!

At the end of a module you will be asked to notice differences. See what has changed, not only with the movement, but also with other aspects of yourself: What is your mind state like now? What other sensations do you notice? Also notice changes as you get up and move around.

A short, simple lesson to give you a feel for what these lessons are like follows. It involves freeing the neck in turning. Before beginning, be sure to read the "grammatical" and movement rules for doing all the lessons in the book.

Grammatical Rules

- All movement directions are in **bold** type.
- All guidance, questions, and repetition numbers are in standard type.

Movement Rules

- If you feel pain, *stop.* Then change either the speed, range, or size of the movement. If this doesn't work, *imagine how it feels to do the movement.*
- Go slowly, do not hurry or become mechanical; you want to *feel* what you are doing.
- Let go of the idea that *trying harder* helps. In a learning situation, such effort gets in the way of feeling what you are doing.
- The number of repetitions suggested is a minimum. Where possible do fifteen to twenty slowly, unless it is a checking movement at the end of a module.
- The pauses are as important as the actions. Do not skip over them.

Illustrations

The illustrations follow the first direction to which they apply. Wait until you have read that direction before looking at and using the illustration. A few illustrations apply to more than one set of directions. In this case the large illustration is for the first direction and the inset is for a later direction. If this is confusing, ignore the illustration.

Where there are black and gray arrows, black indicates where the force is applied and gray represents movement in response to that force.

MINI-ATM: FREEING THE NECK TO TURN FREELY

1. Stand comfortably with your feet shoulder width apart. **Slowly turn your head left and right several times.** Notice how far, how easily, and how smoothly it moves in each direction.

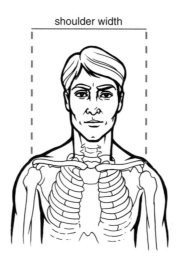

2. **Move your head and shoulders to look to the left and back to the center.** Do this 4 to 6 times. Remember to do this slowly and gently.

3. **Slowly turn just your shoulders toward the left and back to the center, leaving your head facing forward.** Do this 4 to 6 times.

4. **Fix your eyes on a point in front of you. Now turn your head to the left-**

and back to the center, leaving your eyes fixed on that point. Slowly repeat this motion. Move gently so you avoid eyestrain.

5. **Now turn your head left and right slowly.** Compare the ease and distance of your movements to the left to those of your movements to the right. Also compare them to the movements you made when you began.

6. To balance yourself, repeat steps 2 through 4 on the right side.

2

Control and Letting Go

Whenever we engage in an activity, we desire to be in control. We want to know that we are *doing* something, particularly if we are not confident of our skill or ability. So, if we can feel ourselves doing it, whatever it is, we feel we are performing properly. Yet when we are doing something really well, we are so focused there is no sense of anything but enacting our intent. There is an effortless kind of effort that occurs when we truly perform well. This sensation has many names: flow, oneness, the elusive obvious, being "in the zone." But it is replicating the experience, not naming it, that really matters. To replicate the flow state, we have to allow our natural way of being to occur. Thus, active control is anathema to reaching this state. This means that, ultimately, active control gets in the way of optimal performance.

Consider what happens when we endeavor to actively control some area. For a vocalist, this often seems to occur with the jaw, tongue, breath mechanics, or the soft palate. Operating on a preset notion of how that area should perform, we consciously direct it to perform this way. This actually means *forcing* ourselves to perform a particular way. We would not do this if we felt we were performing properly without this force. After a while this sense of forcing becomes habitual, which often leads us to believe that if the force is not there, we are doing something wrong. But this extra effort is wrong! An old joke illustrates this point. An army recruit in basic training has a mother who is a terrible cook. One day he comes running to his drill sergeant yelling, "Sarge! Sarge! Something terrible has happened! Send me to the doc quick." The sergeant looks at him and asks, "What's wrong?" The recruit answers, "My fire's gone out." Seems he'd had heartburn so long that he thought it was normal. In the same way, forcing can become so habitual that we don't know we are doing it until we stop. Whether habitual or not, *a felt sense of force or effort is an indicator of suboptimal performance (i.e., something is wrong).* This is true *even if we get the sound we and the listener want,* because when this occurs, we are using extra effort and/or straining, which ultimately leads to a premature deterioration of vocal ability. (Such strain also almost invariably results in either a sound that most people will not like or problems in registration.)

Feldenkrais referred to this extra effort as "parasitic action" (for a brief discussion of this phenomenon, see Feldenkrais 1985, 85–86). This is action that does not contribute to the desired result. It may be somewhat benign, such as curling the toes when you reach upward. Or it may be injurious, like pulling back with the pelvis as you reach forward with the arm. But even when it is benign, it hinders performance. Because your musculature is linked up to the central nervous system, tension anywhere is in a sense tension everywhere. That is, the interconnectedness of our nervous system results in a minute tightening of our other muscles when we tighten a muscle group. Thus, if something is tightened unnecessarily, it results in slightly more force being needed to perform our intent.

This added effort has three effects: (1) we are more fatigued by performing than we need to be; (2) injuries are more likely; and (3) the sound quality is reduced by the added strain. As fatigue is a function of energy expended versus energy available, obviously, for any given task, the less energy used, the less tired we will be. With extra effort, injuries are more likely both because the extra effort itself leads to added strain and wear and tear and because as we tire, injuries are more likely. As more effort is made, a tense quality envelops the musculature. Since the sound we produce is a product of our entire self, this tense quality colors our sound.

Because both parasitic action and active control involve unnecessary effort, their consequences are the same: fatigue, injury, and a distortion of sound. As the voice ages, there is another consequence: loss of range. This is primarily a function of damage over time (much of which is reversible) brought about by unnecessary strain. Thus, singers who sing with ease tend to last longer and to retain their full range much longer.

This phenomenon of unnecessary effort is actually widespread. Feldenkrais was well aware of this. Hence he often asserted, *"We create our own difficulty."* This is an unusual assertion, but it is true. As you become more familiar with this work, you will be able to verify it from your own experience.

It is not clear to what extent this pattern of creating difficulty is innate or social—nor does it matter. Here, quite simply, is how it works: When you endeavor to do something beyond your capacity, the standard approach is to *try harder*. When you try harder, you tense up. This act of tensing up can actually prevent you from achieving your objective; if you do achieve it, it is at a cost, usually of discomfort. For example, open your mouth a little. This is easy. Now open your mouth while pushing up against the jaw with the left hand. Can you feel how the jaw and neck muscles tighten? Even though you are clear that this is not doable (because of the arm's strength), the impetus is to *try* harder and tighten. Did you notice how uncomfortable this was? When something is perceived as difficult, the same pattern occurs: we tighten up to achieve. This tightening results in both excess tension and a feeling of difficulty. Repeat this pattern enough and many things become difficult. This is one reason why "old" people become restricted. They, in effect, practice doing things with difficulty until they do in fact become difficult. (Math anxiety is another manifestation of this.) It is also why when you have trouble singing a particular piece, after a while it becomes very, very difficult. You've actually practiced doing it wrong (not deliberately, of course) until you've mastered your wrong version. Yet this sense of difficulty is unnecessary. If you can allow yourself to fail with ease, while going in the desired direction, you will find that achieving becomes easier. Eventually you will find a way to do what you want to do. And that way will be a way of ease, especially in contrast to earlier efforts.

ALLOWING OR PASSIVE CONTROL

Allowing yourself to do something well sounds easy. Unfortunately it is not. The problem is finding the place between actively controlling and being lackadaisical. It actually takes a lot of practice and effort to achieve "effortless effort." However, this is practice aimed at letting go of the felt sense of effort while realizing intent. You can think of this as *passive control*, a control achieved by having a clear intent without a sense of force.

The ease found in passive control is related to meditation. In fact, it may be considered a deeply meditative state, one where all of us is involved so deeply that the sense of our self disappears. The same sense occurs when singing well—that is, you lose your "self sense," and it just happens. At the same time, your senses are sharpened. You can feel exactly what you are doing, and minor adjustments often seem to happen by themselves. Of course, you need to practice "letting go" for this to happen with any frequency.

Although we are trained by our society to seek active control, it is this passive control that really allows us the control we want. In this situation, we are able to concentrate on enacting our intent—our real goal—and not controlling, for example, a soft palate or tongue. The latter is a secondary control that we may feel necessary to achieve our true intent, but it is not what we wish to do for its own sake. Also, this giving up of control allows us to use active control, if we feel it necessary, as is sometimes the case when we are injured or ill. This is not an option when we rely on active control.

A good way to begin exploring this concept is letting the floor support our weight. Many people actually think they must hold themselves up. But if you put your weight down into the ground, you will automatically be held up. The following exercise is designed for you to feel this phenomenon.

ATM: WEIGHTS AND LEVERS

This lesson may be done in a chair. In that case do only the first two modules. To do the lesson in a chair, follow the directions but instead of raising your legs, move to the front edge of the chair. When you rest, move back in the chair.

1. Lie on your back. Scan yourself. Where does your back make contact with the floor? How do your buttocks make contact? How balanced do you feel? **Bend your knees so that your feet are on the floor. The way to do this that is easiest on the back is to bend one knee to the side and rotate that leg to standing. Then do the same thing with the other leg. Imagine that there is a piece of paper underneath your right buttock. Raise the buttock into the air by gently shifting the weight down through the left buttock. Raise only far enough to enable you to remove the imaginary piece of paper.** Repeat this 8 or more times. Pause for at least as long as it took you to make this movement before repeating it. See if each time you make this movement you can find a way to make it lighter and easier. Stop and rest.

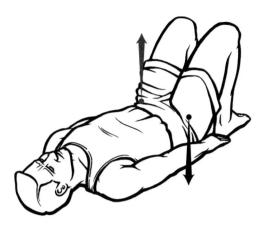

2.   **Another way to lift the right buttock to remove the paper is to put the
     weight down through your right foot.** Do this 4 to 6 times. Each time
     feel how you can make the movement easier. If it helps, imagine a pul-
     ley at the knee joint with a rope tied to the hip and pulled at the foot.
     This will give you a feel for the leverage that is possible. Pause for a
     moment.

3.   Shift the imaginary piece of paper to under the left buttock. **Now shift the
     weight to the right buttock to raise the left.** *Remember to use as little effort
     as possible.* Sense that all that is needed is simply to shift the weight. Repeat
     this at least 8 times. Each time find a way to make the shift lighter.
     Remember to pause between movements to allow the nervous system to
     process. When you feel that you can do this movement lightly and easily,
     stop for a rest.

4.   **Now see what happens when you push through the left foot to lift the
     left buttock.** Do this 5 or 6 times. Remember, lift just enough to remove
     the sheet of paper. Stop. Stretch your legs out and rest. Scan yourself
     and compare how you fit the floor now with how you were when you
     began.

This is the end of this module. If you stop here, pause a moment before standing.
Then stand and notice any changes. Finally, walk a little and notice if it feels different. Resume at step 5.

5. Once more, lie on your back and briefly scan yourself. **Bend your knees and put your feet on the floor. Shift the weight onto the ribs on your left side. You may also move your head to the left some. Allow this weight shift to raise the right buttock up enough to remove the sheet of paper.** Repeat this at least 5 times until the movement feels graceful. If it still feels a little forced after 10 repetitions, stop. A sense of ease will be there when you try this again later. Pause.

6. **Now lift the left buttock using the same procedure. Now it is the ribs on the right side that are weighted.** Again aim for a feeling of grace and ease. Do not force it. If you force a movement, you only learn force. You do not become more proficient. Repeat this movement 5 to 10 times. Then stop for a moment.

7. **Now combine weighting the right side of the pelvis and the left foot to lift the left buttock.** Do this 3 or 4 times. How is this different from using just one of these methods?

    Add in weighting the ribs. Do this another 3 or 4 times. Can you tell that all three were involved earlier, with one dominant and the other two happening because they *must* happen to make this movement? Rest for a moment.

8. **Raise the left buttock by combining any two of the three orientations you did earlier.** Do this 3 or 4 times.

    Now add in the third and repeat 3 or 4 times. Stop. Stretch your legs out. Scan yourself and compare how you fit the floor now with how you fit when you began.

This is the end of this module. If you stop here, pause a moment before standing. Then stand and notice any changes. Finally, walk a little and notice if it feels different. This ends the chair version of this lesson. Resume at step 9 for the floor version.

---

9. **Lie on your back with your legs out straight. In this position put the weight down through your right buttock to lift the left buttock the way**

you did before. This will be more difficult than before, but do not use force. Use only the minimum weight shift that you need to lift the buttock. Do this 4 or 5 times. Pause.

10. **Now do the same movement on the other side, so that the right buttock lifts.** Repeat 4 or 5 times. Each time allow the movement to be softer and gentler. Rest a moment.

11. **Find a way to put weight down through your right leg, and particularly your right heel, to lift the right buttock.** Each time you do this, be a bit kinder to yourself. The movement requires considerable concentration, especially at first, but not great power. Find out how well you can substitute finesse for power as you repeat this movement. Do it at least 5 and as many as 9 times. Rest a moment.

12. **Repeat step 11 on the other side.** Do it 5 to 7 times. Remember to aim for greater ease each time. Are you pausing between movements for as long as it takes to make the movement, or have you begun to rush and get mechanical? Rest a moment.

13. **Bend your knees and put your feet flat on the floor. Try lifting first the right buttock and then the left buttock using the easiest way.** Has it changed since the last time? Rest.

This is the end of this module. If you stop here, pause a moment before standing. Then stand and notice any changes. Finally walk a little and notice differences. Resume at step 14.

---

14. **Lie flat with your legs stretched out. Move the weight through the ribs on the left to raise the right buttock. Allow your head to roll. Do not worry if the pelvis doesn't lift much or at all. Just make the weight shift.** Do it 5 to 7 times, each time listening to the movement to find out if it is more complete. Rest.

15. **Repeat the prior movement, only move the weight to the right.** Do it 4 to 6 times *gently*. Pause.

16. **Combine all three ways of weight shifting to lift the left buttock.** Do it 3 times. **Then lift the right buttock 3 times, shifting the weight the other way. Finally go back and forth 2 times.** Rest, noticing your contact with the floor.

17. **Bend your legs so that your feet are on the floor. Alternate between lifting the left and right buttock.** Compare it to earlier. Pause, come to sitting and standing. Notice any changes. Walk a little. How balanced does it feel? Do you notice any differences?

END OF LESSON

TENSION AND FUNCTION

Tension is necessary to life. Without any tonus (muscle tension) we cannot stand, sit, or even breathe. Problems arise when tension is excessive, misplaced, or insufficient. If we use more tension than needed to perform any task, that performance will seem strained. We will sense that extra effort is involved. For example, you do not need to clench your jaw while reading this. But do so anyway. Can you feel the sense of strain? Notice your feet while you do this. Do you feel that even they are now slightly tensed? This is what extra (or unnecessary) effort does to us. Over time this extra effort also results in needless wear and tear. Sometimes we do not tense all over but add extra tension in an area that does not further our intent. This has the same result as generalized excessive tension. If you did the jaw-clenching exercise, you have already felt this. If we are persistently tensed, after a while we often do not feel this strain. It becomes so habitual that we consider it our normal way of being. But a trained observer will notice it. When we are singing, the strain will manifest itself in our sound. Unless it is very slight, this impact on our sound will be noticeable. It results in a constricted, less pleasing sound. There are also often restrictions of range and a muddying of diction. Over time the voice deteriorates needlessly.

Insufficient tension also reduces the capacity to produce sound. Without tension, there is no sound, such as with a slack violin or guitar string. However, this is not as common a problem. It usually occurs when the voice is fatigued or overworked, in young girls' voices, or when the singer is trying to employ a "breathy" sound.

We wish, therefore, to walk the tightrope of ideal tension—just enough to perform and no more. At first, this is difficult. However, as we develop a feel for keeping proper tension, doing so becomes easier, although it still requires us to remain focused. The ideal is to make appropriate tension habitual. When we do so, performing becomes comfortable and has a graceful, easy feel to all involved.

The following lesson will give you a chance to explore relative tension levels. You will be able to experience what is excessive and also how much you need to do to enact your intent.

ATM: TAMING TONGUE TENSION

1. Sit comfortably (or lie on your back with your knees bent and your feet on the floor or stretched out). **Open your mouth and see how this feels.** Repeat several times and see if you can make this easier each time.

    Make soft fists with your hands and release them several times. Allow your hands to feel freer and more relaxed each time. Now open your mouth again and see how this feels.

2. Move your tongue to the lower right-hand corner of your mouth. **Touch the inside of the tooth furthest back in your mouth that you can reach easily. Then move up and touch the top of this tooth.** Is it still easy? If not, move the tongue closer to the center of the mouth until you are touching the tooth *without strain. Do not go further with your tongue than you can go with ease.* Many people can touch the inside of their last molar, but when they move to the top there is a slight sense of strain. **If this is so, move to the next tooth.** Explore the top of this tooth. What does this feel like?

    Go to each tooth in turn until you have gone as far to the left side of your mouth as you can *comfortably*. Pause and rest for a moment.

3. **Touch the tooth furthest back in the lower right-hand corner of your mouth that you can reach comfortably.** Explore the inside surface of this tooth. *Be certain that you are doing this without strain. Sense clearly the tiniest*

strain and find a way to reduce it. If this means moving closer to the center of your mouth, do so.

Go to each tooth in turn and explore its inside surface, without strain, until you have gone as far to the left as you can comfortably. Pause.

Open your mouth. Can you feel a difference between the upper and lower area of your mouth? Rest.

4.   **Touch the tooth furthest back in the upper right-hand corner of your mouth that you can *comfortably reach* with your tongue. Move the tongue and touch the top of this tooth.** If you feel any strain, even the slightest, move to the next tooth toward the center. Explore the top of this tooth. Notice the peaks and valleys. If you have fillings, see if you can feel the difference in the texture.

Examine the next tooth with your tongue. Continue to explore the top of each tooth moving to your left until you reach either the last tooth on the left or begin to experience tension in the tongue. Pause and rest for a moment.

5.   **Touch the tooth furthest back in the upper right-hand corner of your mouth that you can reach comfortably.** Explore the back surface of this tooth. What shape is your tongue in as you do this? Can you sense the area where the tongue feels at ease? Allow this sense of ease to spread and to develop as you perform the following movement.

Go to each tooth in turn and explore its inside, without strain, until you have gone as far to the left as you can comfortably. Pause.

Open your mouth. Compare the way this feels now to how it felt when you began.

This is the end of this module. It is a logical place to stop if you cannot do the lesson in one sitting. Resume at step 6.

---

6.   **Open your mouth twice. Reach over your lower teeth with your tongue and touch the outside surface of the tooth furthest in the right rear that you can reach comfortably.** You will now be using the underside of your tongue to explore your tooth. **Explore this tooth and then continue toward the center and left. Go only as far as you can comfortably.** Do not hurry. Going slowly allows you to feel each surface and the spaces between teeth. **When you have gone as far as you can to the left, bring your tongue back inside the teeth.** Pause and rest.

7.   **Now touch the upper front surface of your teeth with your tongue as far to the right rear as you can.** This time you are using the front of your tongue. **Explore this tooth and continue toward the center and the left. Go as fast as you can provided that you feel the entire surface and you do not increase the tension in your tongue.** Can you feel the difference in the shape of your teeth as you proceed from molars to incisors? How does the bend in your tongue change as you proceed around? **When you have reached your comfortable limit on the left, return your tongue to its normal location.** Pause and rest.

8.   **Open your mouth.** What is it like now?

       Now touch the lower front surface of your teeth with your tongue as far to the right rear as you can. Move your tongue to the left until you reach the furthest tooth on the lower left. Then move up to the upper. Move from left to right across the upper teeth. When you get to the furthest right you can, move down and begin again. Make 2 circular movements. **Imagine making this circular movement twice more.** See if you can imagine the movement being a little smoother. **Now actually do the movement again.** How is it now? Pause very briefly.

       Now reverse the direction. Make another 4 or 5 circular movements. Pause. **Open your mouth and feel what it is like now.**

This is the end of this module. It is a logical place to stop if you cannot do the lesson in one sitting. Resume at step 9.

---

9.   **Open your mouth.** What does it feel like to open it now?

Open your mouth, reach out with your tongue, and touch the center of your lower lip. Repeat this 5 or 6 times, making the touch softer each time.

Now touch the center of your upper lip with your tongue. Repeat 5 or 6 times; each time do it a little more slowly. Pause.

Touch the right corner of your mouth with your tongue. Repeat 5 or 6 times. Do you mostly curve your tongue or move from the base of the tongue to reach this corner?

Open your mouth. Is there a difference between sides?

Touch the left corner of your mouth with your tongue. Repeat 5 or 6 times. Pause and rest.

10. **Open your mouth, reach out with your tongue, touch the center of your lower lip, and stay there briefly. Then proceed to move your tongue** *slowly* **around your lips to the right.** Notice the differences in texture as you move to the corners. Do you feel any bumps or cracks as you move around the lips? Repeat 5 or 6 times.

Now reverse direction. What feels different about this direction? Repeat 5 or 6 times. Pause and rest.

11. **Open your mouth.** What is it like now?

Touch the inside of the tooth furthest back in the lower right-hand corner of your mouth that you can reach comfortably. Move the tongue up and across the upper teeth. Then move down and back to the right. Repeat this circular motion 4 or 5 times. Notice how the tongue is "jammed up" a bit in this movement. Can you still keep this movement soft?

Now reverse the direction. Repeat 4 or 5 times and pause. **Open your mouth.** What is it like now?

12. **Now try a few movements of the tongue around the lips. Pause and reverse direction.** Repeat 3 or 4 times.

   Open your mouth. How did the movement feel this time? How does your tongue feel?

END OF LESSON

3

The Base of Support

THE ROLE OF FEET AND LEGS

The feet and legs form the crucial base of support for singing. This is true of sitting as well as standing. Clearly, you can't sing if you jump and try to keep your feet off the ground. But try singing with your feet in the air while seated. It is an enormous strain. No one, therefore, performs or advocates singing in this position. Though your feet and legs are vitally important to singing your best, not much time or effort is spent on their proper use and care. Learning to use your feet well is often the quickest and easiest way to noticeably improve your singing.

Maximum stability and support are achieved when both feet are firmly on the floor. In this situation the weight is approximately evenly distributed between the two because no one uses their two sides completely evenly. Indeed, our two sides are usually somewhat different in weight, width, height (at shoulder level), and even depth. In some people the difference is so pronounced that they need different shoe sizes for their two feet. However, when we are in balance, the weight will be distributed between our two legs in accordance with the proportions of our sides. That is, if one side is 2 percent bigger than the other, then that leg will, on average, carry 2 percent more weight.

When the weight is not even, we lean to one side or the other. This compresses the ribs on one side, compromising our breathing. There is also some compression in the neck that impinges on the larynx. Uneven leg length is one common cause of improper weight distribution. This can often be spotted because the person will equalize the weight by having one foot (the long leg) forward of the other. If the discrepancy is small (0.6 centimeter, or 1/4 inch, or less) this can be accommodated functionally. That is, how we use ourselves, especially how we curve our spine, allows us to accommodate these relatively small differences without strain. A lift is necessary to properly handle discrepancies of up to about an inch. Greater discrepancies require adaptive shoes. Usually people who stand with the same leg clearly forward of the other versus parallel or alternating the forward leg have a noticeable leg-length differential. If this does not sound like you, go to the next paragraph. A section at the end of this chapter is devoted to leg-length differentials.

Balance is not a stationary phenomenon. It is a dynamic event. We must remain in balance whenever we shift our weight, and, clearly, we must remain in balance when moving. Otherwise we would fall instead of being able to walk, run, ski, and so on. But even when standing, we are constantly shifting our weight. No one stands stock-still for long, not even the queen of England's guardsmen. The goal is to always be able to shift one's weight easily in any direction. When we can shift easily, we feel secure and in balance. Whenever we are unbalanced, our rib cage is not being properly supported, and we have a feeling of insecurity. And when we feel insecure, we tend to both tighten up and hold our breath. The net result is that we diminish our performance.

It is one of life's paradoxes that we often adopt a strategy that backfires. For example, when we feel unstable, we tense up to prevent ourselves from falling. But that very tensing makes us less stable. Of course, there is some sense in this phenomenon. If we truly are falling, stiffening ourselves to grab on to something often works. But to remain in this holding-on mode when we are not falling is self-defeating. It restricts the ability to flow with changes, putting us out of balance repeatedly. Being out of balance compels us to tighten some muscles to remain upright, move, etc. That we are tightening these muscles more than necessary is both unfortunate and an opportunity. Unfortunate, because it leaves us performing below our potential. An opportunity, because as we learn to be in better balance so that we more closely approach using minimum necessary force, we will feel and perform better.

How can you tell whether you are really in balance? Clearly, if you feel like you are falling, you have lost your balance. But good balance is much subtler than not falling. Often we are a little out of balance and compensate by using extra effort or a suboptimal alignment. Standing with one leg forward to compensate for a leg-length differential is an example of suboptimal alignment. A simple way to see if you are out of balance (or how much) is to see whether you can readily move in all directions. If one leg is forward, you are already committed in that direction. You cannot move further that way without rearranging yourself. At a minimum you have to move your weight onto the back leg to advance your forward leg at all. Statically how much you are out of balance can be gauged by how much, if any, preliminary weight shift you have to make to move in a direction. This will change from moment to moment because we are not static. As long as we are alive, we are in constant movement (however small). Therefore dynamic balance is crucial. Dynamic balance occurs when our pattern moves us through the position that facilitates movement in all directions most of the time. Think of your central position as home base. When you are in dynamic balance, home base is a position that allows easy movement in any direction. When you are going out from, and then returning through, a dynamic home base, you achieve a sense of balance.

The following lesson is aimed at establishing and retaining a dynamic sense of balance.

ATM: Balance in Standing

1. Stand with your feet shoulder width apart. If practical to do so, take off your shoes. Have a chair or other support available to place one of your hands on. How does this feel? Do you feel balanced? Supported? **Shift your weight (pelvis) left and right several times.** How evenly did you do this? How easy was this?

    Move your weight forward and back several times. Pause.

2. **Place your right foot directly in front of your left foot, if possible. Place your hand on the chair back if you need to maintain your stability. Put most of your weight on your left foot. Now shift your weight to the front of your left foot and then back to the center.** Repeat this shift at least 5 times. Then pause with your weight still on the center of your left foot.

    Shift your weight to the rear of your left foot and then back to the center. Repeat this at least 5 times. Pause and balance the weight between the two feet for a moment.

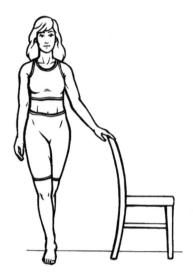

3. **Put most of your weight on your left foot. Shift the weight from the front to the rear of your foot.** Repeat this 7 to 9 times. Where are you shifting weight? Do several of the above shifts with the pelvis and a few concentrating on the ankle. What feels best to you? **Pause. Put your right foot parallel to the left and rest a minute.** Which leg seems to support you better?

4. **Place your right foot directly in front of your left foot. Again, if you need to, place your hand on the chair for stability. Put most of your weight on your right foot. Shift your weight to the back of the right foot and then back to its center.** Repeat this shift at least 5 times. Pause.

    Shift your weight to the front of your right foot and then back to the center. Repeat this at least 5 times. Pause and balance the weight between the two feet for a moment.

5. **Put most of your weight on your right foot. Shift the weight from the front to the rear of your foot.** Repeat this 7 to 9 times. Notice how you do this and try at least one other way. Put your right foot parallel with the left.

    Move forward and back a few times. How does this feel now? Pause and rest for a moment.

This is the end of this module. It is a logical place to stop if you cannot do the lesson in one sitting. Resume at step 6.

6.   **Place your right foot directly in front of your left foot. Put your weight on your left foot. Move the weight to the outside of the left foot and back to the center.** Repeat this at least 5 times and then pause with the weight in the center.

   Now move the weight onto the left foot. Shift it from the center to the inside and back. Repeat this 5 to 7 times. Rest with your feet parallel to each other.

7.   **Place your right foot in front of your left foot. Put your weight on your left foot. Move the weight forward and then make a circle with your weight over the foot.** Repeat this at least 5 times. Note the direction you chose. Recall how this feels.

   Reverse direction. Circle at least 5 times. Is this as easy as the other direction? Usually we choose the easiest route without even thinking about it. Stop.

   Place your feet side by side. Move your pelvis left and right a few times. Is it easier to go in one direction? Rest for a minute.

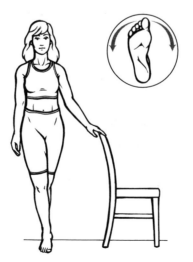

8. **Place your right foot directly in front of your left foot. Put your weight on your right foot. Move the weight to the inside of the right foot and back to the center.** Repeat this at least 5 times and then pause with the weight in the center.

    Move the weight onto the right foot. Move the weight to the outside of the foot and back. Repeat this 4 to 6 times. Rest with your feet parallel to each other.

9. **Place your right foot in front of your left foot. Put the weight on the right foot. Make a circle with your weight over the foot.** Repeat at least 5 times. Allow the circle to be rounder each time.

    Reverse direction. Repeat at least 5 times. Is this circle as round as the one in the other direction? Stop.

    Place your feet side by side. Move your pelvis forward and back. Pause. Compare this to when you began. **Move side to side.** Compare this to how it was initially. Stop for a minute.

This is the end of this module. It is a logical place to stop if you cannot do the lesson in one sitting. Resume at step 10.

---

10. **Place your left foot in front of your right foot. Place a hand on a chair if you need support. Put the weight on the right foot. Move the weight from the center to the front of the foot. Now move the weight from the front through the center to the back of the foot and back.** Repeat this 10 times. Go slower and slower each time. Pause.

11. **Put your weight onto your right foot. Move the weight to the inside of the right foot then back through the center to the outside. Go back and forth from the inside of the foot to the outside.** Repeat this 10 times. Does this weight shift become easier each time? Pause, place your feet parallel to each other, and rest a minute. Notice any differences between your right and left sides. Pay special attention to differences between your two feet.

12. **Place your left foot in front of your right foot. Put the weight onto the left foot. Move the weight from the center to the front of the foot. Next move the weight to the back of the foot and then return to the front.** Repeat this 10 times. Notice where you shift your weight and explore shifting from other places. Pause.

13. **Put your weight onto your left foot. Move the weight to the inside of the left foot then back through the center to the outside. Go back and forth from the inside of the foot to the outside.** Repeat this 10 times. See how gentle you can be with yourself as you do this. Pause.

    Place your feet side by side. Move forward and back. How is this compared to when you began? Pause and rest for a minute. Notice how balanced you feel. Compare this to when you began.

This is the end of this module. It is a logical place to stop if you cannot do the lesson in one sitting. Resume at step 14.

---

14. **Place your left foot in front of your right foot. Put the weight onto the left foot. Move the weight from the front to the back of the left foot twice.** Pause.

    Now move the weight between the inside and the outside of the foot twice. Pause.

    Make a circle with the weight on the left foot. Notice the direction of this circle. Go around 7 to 9 times. See if you can make each movement more circular or easier. Pause.

    Make a circle in the opposite direction to the one you just made. Go around at least 6 times. Pause and place your feet parallel. Rest a minute.

15. **Place your left foot in front of your right foot. Put the weight onto the right foot. Move the weight from the front to the back of the right foot twice.** Pause.

Now move the weight from the inside to the outside of the foot twice. Pause.

Make a circle with the weight on the right foot. Go around 7 to 9 times. Pause.

Make a circle in the opposite direction to the one you just made. Go around at least 6 times. Pause and place your feet parallel. Rest a minute.

16. Imagine that you are trying to balance a plate on your head. **Make a circle with your pelvis without moving either your head or your feet.** Go around 5 to 7 times. Pause.

Now make a circle in the opposite direction. Go around at least 6 times. Pause. Notice how balanced you feel now.

Move your weight forward and back several times. Compare to when you began. Pause.

Move your weight left and right. Again compare with how it was initially. Stop and rest a minute. Then walk and observe how you feel. Note your balance from time to time as you resume your normal activities.

END OF LESSON

USING THE FLOOR

Just as the weight should be distributed evenly between the legs, it also should be distributed evenly over the foot. That is, roughly half the weight is on the front and back, and roughly half is inside (the big toe) and outside. When the weight distribution at home base is too much in any direction, it distorts and weakens the singing voice. Too much weight on the front of the foot pushes you into overextension. It also gives you the feeling that you might pitch forward. Moreover, it results in a thinner sound by impairing the breathing (see "High Heels," p. 46, for details). If the weight is too far back on the heels, you will feel unsupported as if the chest is behind the pelvis. This makes it more difficult to open your ribs to breathe, and you will have difficulty projecting.

If you tend to collapse to the inside (flat-footedness is the extreme), there is a tightness in the buttocks. This will make it more difficult to open your ribs to the side. You will also have a stretched sensation in the neck. As a result, you will have trouble fully opening up both your breathing and your larynx. Strengthening your arch will reduce the tendency to collapse to the inside. Strengthening the adductors, the muscles that hold your thighs together, can help strengthen your arch. The thigh-strengthening exercise at the end of the chapter will help strengthen the adductors.

If the weight is too far to the outside, the buttocks will be squeezed tight. This will make it harder to open the ribs in back.

The following lesson is designed to teach you what it feels like to have a more even weight distribution on the feet. It also will help you feel that the best position for the feet in sitting (provided you fit the chair) is with your knees over your ankles.

ATM: The Connection of Feet Through to Head

1. Take your shoes off. Sit forward comfortably on the edge of the chair. Have your feet in front of you, shoulder width apart. **Keeping the ball of your right foot on the floor, lift your right heel from the floor a couple times.** How easy is it?

   Now lift the ball of the right foot several times. Is it easier or harder than lifting the heel? Notice the relationship of the knee to the ankle. **Move your leg forward so that the ankle is in front of the knee.** (If you dropped a line from your knee, the ankle would be in front of it.) **Alternate lifting the heel and the ball of the foot several times.** Which movement is easier than before, which harder?

   Now move the leg so that the ankle is behind the knee. Alternate lifting the heel and the ball of the foot, once or twice only, very slowly. Has the ball of your foot become quite difficult to lift?

Now move the leg forward until the ankle is under the knee. Alternate lifting the ball and the heel. Is it easier to go back and forth in this position than in the others?

Move your foot a little forward and back until you find the best place for both movements. Where is it? Compare the relationship of the right knee and ankle to that of the left. Pause and notice how your left and right sides line up.

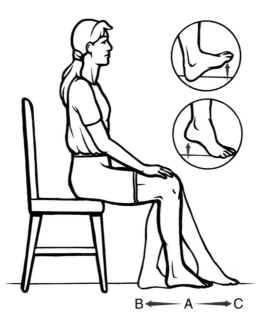

2.   **Now lift your left heel a number of times.**

Then lift the ball of the foot several times. Move the foot forward and back a little into several different positions, alternating lifting the heel and the ball of the foot in each. Find the position where the combined movements seem easiest. Compare this placement with that of the right leg.

3.   **Alternating right and left feet, lift the heel and the ball of each foot.** Do this 4 times. Compare the way your two sides feel. Stand and walk a little.

This is the end of this module. It is a logical place to stop if you cannot do the lesson in one sitting. Resume at step 4.

4.   Sit forward on the edge of your chair and remember how your feet were positioned at the end of the previous lesson module. **Alternate lifting the heel and the ball of each foot several times to see if this still feels relatively easy. If not, adjust the position of the leg.**

5.   **Now lift the inside of your left foot slowly several times. Then lift the right hip.** Gently repeat this movement 3 or 4 times.

      Explore lifting the inside of the left foot now. Is it easier than before?

      Add lifting the right hip to lifting the inside of the left foot. Do this 3 or 4 times. **Then go back and just lift the inside of the foot.** Slowly sit back in your seat and compare the way the two feet fit on the floor.

6.   **Move forward again and lift the inside of the right foot several times.** What does your head do?

      Now lift the left hip several times as you raise the inside of the right foot. What do you notice about the way your head moves now?

Then lift the inside of the right foot by itself. Pause and compare sides.

7.   **Alternate lifting the right and then the left hip slowly.** Repeat this 5 or 6 times.

Then alternate lifting the inside of the left and right feet 5 or 6 times. Pause; notice how your feet are on the ground.

Stand for a moment and be aware of the feeling. Now walk for a minute.

This is the end of this module. It is a logical place to stop if you cannot do the lesson in one sitting. Resume at step 8.

---

8.   Sit comfortably forward on the edge of the chair. **Lift the heel and ball of each foot a few times to check ease of movement and the position of the foot.** Recall the last module. Remember lifting the inside of each foot.

Once again alternate, lifting first the left and then the right hip 4 or 5 times.

9.   **Lift the outside of the right foot 6 to 8 times.** What happens in the pelvis when you do this? What do you do with your head? (Note: Some people will move the head to the left a little, others to the right. There is no *correct* way; we just want to draw attention to the relationship.)

Alternate lifting the inside and the outside of the right foot 5 or 6 times. Sit back and rest. While you do so, compare your two sides.

10.   Come forward in your chair. **Now lift the outside of the left foot 6 to 8 times.** What happens in the pelvis when you do this? Do you feel the same effect with the head as when you lifted the outside of the right foot, or is it the opposite?

Now alternate lifting the outside and the inside of the left foot several

times. How do your feet feel against the floor now? How balanced do you feel on the chair?

Stand and notice how this feels. Walk a little. What is it like?

This is the end of this module. It is a logical place to stop if you cannot do the lesson in one sitting. Resume at step 11.

---

11. Sit comfortably on the edge of the chair. Recall alternately lifting the heel and the toe of each foot. **Repeat each motion several times.**

     Now alternate lifting the left and the right hip 2 times. How does that feel today?

     Lift the inside and the outside of the right foot 4 times. Pause.

     Now lift the inside and the outside of the left foot 3 times. Pause.

12. **Slowly lift the right heel. As you put the heel down, raise the inside of the right foot. As you put the inside of the foot down, lift the ball of the foot. Now as you put the ball down, lift the outside of the right foot.** You have now, in effect, made a circle with the foot against the floor. Slowly continue to circle in this manner for at least 4 revolutions. Can you allow the movement to become easier? Maybe if you make it smaller, it would be easier.

     Now reverse direction. Again go around at least 4 times. What do you notice in your hips as you make this circle? Do you feel any effects of this movement in the position of the head? Stop. Compare the way the left and right feet feel against the floor. Does either foot feel better connected to the back, to the head? Rest.

13. Come forward in your chair. **Now begin making circles with your left foot. Go in the direction you choose. After each circle, pause a moment.**

Then change either the size, the effort, or the speed at which you do the next circle. What is the relation between size and effort, speed and effort? Make at least 5 circles. How attentive are you if you go faster?

Now reverse the direction. Go slowly and easily, endeavoring to make this circle seem effortless. As it becomes less effortful, do you feel more or less of yourself involved in the movement? When you sense that all of you is involved in the movement, make one more circle and stop. How do your feet feel against the floor now? How are you sitting in the chair? Do you feel any shift in your sense of the way the feet support the head?

Stand up and walk around for a moment. Notice what this feels like now. How easy is walking now compared to when you began? How much can you feel your feet as you walk now?

END OF LESSON

HIGH HEELS

Wearing platform or stiletto heels is a good way to impair your breathing and produce a thinner sound. Elevating the heels unduly occurs when the heel is higher than the toe by more than about 1 inch or 2.5 centimeters. Heels of this height distort the position of the spine, throwing one into an overextension (lordosis). The belly is pushed forward, the chest back, the chin up, and the larynx slightly back. Internally, this results in a narrowing of the vocal channel and reduction of the ability to carry air. You can feel this for yourself. Stand barefoot and notice how you are breathing and the sense of ease in your throat. Now go up on tiptoes as high as you can comfortably. What is the sense of ease in your throat relative to what it was with heels down? How free is your breath? In general, the higher the heel, the greater the distortion. However, stiletto heels are worse than platforms because they are unstable. In addition to being thrown into extension, there is also the question of keeping one's balance. Therefore, avoid high heels whenever possible. And when you *must* wear them, keep them as low as possible and try to wear platform, not stiletto, heels.

LEG-LENGTH DIFFERENTIAL

With an acute enough measuring device, we would find that none of us have even leg lengths. In fact, most people have a difference of at least 1/16 of an inch. In one study of 100 asymptomatic soldiers, 71 had a leg-length differential of at least 1/16 of an inch, while 33 had a difference of at least 3/16 of an inch. In a study of 1,446 schoolchildren ages five to seventeen, 80 percent had a discrepancy of at least 1/16 of an inch. (See Travell and Simons 1983, 1: 104–8, for a more complete discussion of leg-length differentials.) This lesser leg length imposes a strain on the musculature, because the muscles attempt to correct the resulting distortions in alignment to maintain level head and shoulders. Two other conditions may mimic, compensate for, or add to a leg-length difference. These are a tilting of the sacrum relative to the pelvis and an abrupt lateral angulation in the spine. Because of these factors and the human organism's overall capacity to accommodate, differences of less than 1/4 of an inch are not considered functionally significant for pain creation.

We are capable of accommodating significant differentials without discomfort. A great amount of research has been done on leg-length differential and pain. According to Travell and Simons, a differential of 1.3 centimeters (1/2 inch) may cause no pain symptoms in a lifetime, provided there is no traumatic event that interferes with the person's ability to compensate for the differential. Because of the strain the leg-length difference puts on the sacroiliac and back, back pain is the common response to this difference. Once a pain problem has been created, discrepancies of 3/16 of an inch or more can perpetuate the problem. A study of 443 back patients concluded that a difference of 1/4 inch or more should be corrected with a heel lift.

In another experiment, a pain-free, normal individual had a 3/4-inch elevation added to the heel of the left shoe. On the third day, the subject experienced aching in the buttocks. After three weeks, there was regular night pain in the back and buttocks. When the elevation was removed, the symptoms disappeared in two weeks.

> Gross queried a group of patients with a short leg, regardless of symptoms and found that those with a discrepancy of 9/16 of an inch or less, did not regard their short leg as a problem, did not wear a lift, and did not feel unbalanced. However, those who had discrepancies of 2.0 cm (3/4 inch) and more responded positively to all of these questions. . . .

In our experience, even in the absence of symptoms, correction of a leg length disparity of 1.3 cm or more is of preventive value. . . . When repeated measurements consistently show a discrepancy of 0.5cm (3/16 in) or more in a patient with low back pain, it should be corrected. (Travell and Simons 1983, 1: 106)

Interestingly, leg-length discrepancies of up to 1.9 centimeters (3/4 inch) are likely to disappear in growing children *if* leg length is equalized temporarily.

What does this mean for vocalists? Clearly, a leg-length difference that will lead to pain should be corrected with a lift. Pain impedes breathing and interferes with vocal performance (as well as making life miserable). What about lesser differences where there is no pain? One way to accommodate is to place the long leg forward. This is why many singers prefer this position and find it stable. Another is to experiment with a slight heel lift to see whether that helps or hinders vocal performance and comfort. No one has really looked into the impact of leg-length differences and voice, so we cannot do more than suggest experimenting until you find what is right for you.

A SIMPLE EXERCISE: STRENGTHENING THE ADDUCTORS

Get a belt and a four- to six-inch hard cushion. Put the cushion between your thighs. Adjust the belt so that it is about twelve inches in diameter. Put the belt over your ankles. Squeeze in on the cushion while simultaneously pressing out with your ankles. Do this for about ten seconds. Relax for thirty to sixty seconds and repeat two or three more times. You may do this exercise several times a day if you enjoy it. You can also increase the time of squeezing as you get stronger if ten seconds seems too brief. Or you might also squeeze a little harder.

4

Intentionality and Effort

INTENTION

One of Moshe Feldenkrais's dicta is that if your intention is clear, you will achieve the result you intend. One reason for this is simple. If you don't know what you intend, you are certain not to get it. Another, more important reason is that developing intent is the function of our conceptual consciousness, to make clear choices as to what we intend. This is what allows us to accomplish what we set out to do. However, conceptual consciousness can only handle one thing at a time. Think about the color of your shirt and what you had for breakfast simultaneously. Can you do it? Or do they come into your consciousness sequentially? Yet, to function, we must be doing many things: breathing, pumping blood, moving our arms, moving our legs. And many of these must be done simultaneously. Some we can volitionally control and some not. But, at any given time, we predominantly operate on automatic pilot, as it were. Moreover, most of the information we receive is also handled outside our conceptual consciousness. When we are clear on our intent, all this automatic functioning facilitates the enactment of our intent. If we are unclear, other possibilities intrude, and we often fail—thus the importance of clear intention.

Indeed, research shows that most of what we do must necessarily be done without thought. Our brain is divided into seven structures, only one of which, the cerebral cortex, is involved with what we consider thinking and voluntary control of musculature. More important than structures in understanding the relationship of thought to action is information flow. This was investigated in the late 1950s, when it was concluded that maximal information flow of the process of conscious sensory perception is about 40 bits per second. Meanwhile we receive over 11 million bits per second from our external receptors, 10 million of which come from the eyes. And yet more information is pouring in from other sensory means, such as the vestibular system, which maintains balance, and proprioception, which is how we know where a body part is without being able to see it. All in all, we are aware of about one-millionth of the information pouring in.

The flow of information measured in bits per second is described as the bandwidth, or capacity, of consciousness. The bandwidth of consciousness is so low relative to the information pouring in, it as if it were a spotlight dramatically illuminating the face of one actor among a vast panoply of characters in an epic. The spotlight can of course move, but it would take a very long time to illuminate all the actors, and in that time they would all have changed position.

There is another difficulty with conscious control. Not only is the bandwidth of consciousness narrow, but also there is a time delay of 0.5 seconds in transmission. That means that you are reacting to past information when you rely on conscious controls. In many cases, such as conversation, this does not matter. However, no one would survive split-second situations if consciousness were always in charge. And in fact it is not. In these situations we are capable of reacting very fast, because a clear intent is (or was) formed and we drop the conscious self and just react. (For more on information flow and the time delay in consciousness, see Norretranders 1998.)

Of course, to enact a clear intent, you must know what you are doing. Another of Feldenkrais's dicta is that if you know what you are doing, you can get what you want. It is important, therefore, to learn what you need to do in order to do what you want and to know what this is. Equally important is to know what you don't need to know. It is easy to think that knowing what you are doing means being aware of everything you do. But this is impossible and, therefore, is a trap, the trap of being overly attentive—or, more accurately, being overly attentive to what we do instead of what we intend. The brain's capacity to organize our movement so that we no longer need to think about it is truly amazing. We take the simple act of walking for granted. But how exactly do you do it? What muscles do you move when? You would have to spend a great deal of time studying this simple act to know the answer to this question academically. To do it in real time would probably prove a severe strain on your bladder (unless you camped out a few feet from a bathroom). And this is true of all but the simplest acts. We cannot be aware of all that is going on. Rather, we must focus our intent and rely on our internal sense of proper functioning to perform.

EFFORTING

To do anything well takes practice and effort, so we are often told to practice more or try harder. Unfortunately, we can practice too much or try too hard. We refer to this overtrying as *efforting*. Many repetitive-strain injuries result from overpracticing. And we can try too hard. Of course, sometimes all it takes to accomplish something is a little more effort, so it is tempting to try a little harder. Unfortunately, too often we get tight when we do this.

It is rather like the old story about the master guitarist teaching his student with only one string on the guitar. The student asks him how can he learn to play with only one string.

"See how it sounds," says the teacher.

The student strums it and nothing happens. No sound.

"It is too slack," says the student to the teacher. "I can get no sound."

"Okay, then give it to me." The teacher makes an adjustment and hands the instrument back.

The student strums it and it squeaks.

"It is too tight, " says the student.

"Okay, " says the teacher. "Adjust it until it is just right. Then you will know how to begin to play."

Actually there is an important difference between trying and doing. Trying is an effort to accomplish something. Doing is the accomplishment of something. In a real sense when we *try* to do a task, it is an acknowledgment that we really do not think we can do it. If we felt we could do it, we just would. It is, in effect, constipation of effort. We once performed an interesting experiment to demonstrate this. We had a student try to walk. As she began to move forward, she was told she wasn't trying, she was walking. As long as she moved, she was still walking. It was only when she stood, didn't move, and yet used effort as if to move that she was really trying. Of course such nonproductive effort is harmful.

What is productive effort, then? Curiously, it is best described by the Zen term of "effortless effort." That is, the effort *is* being put forth. The task *is* being accomplished. But there is no internal feeling of effort. Rather, you are just doing. Other names for this phenomenon are "flow," "being in the groove," and "unconscious." It is a state that we cannot volitionally enter. But we can prepare for it, by attending to how we do what we do and finding easier, gentler, and more effective ways to do it.

POWER AND POTENTIAL

There is another type of effort, one of which we are somewhat unaware: our habitual effort. For any given posture or movement by an individual, there is an absolute minimum of effort and tension required. Because we live in an imperfect world, none of us achieves this minimum. We can only more or less closely approximate it. In particular, we all use excess muscular effort in our habitual posture. It creeps in as we try to achieve, or as we do something and then do not release all the tension we have embodied to perform the task. This excess tension is a particular problem if we repeatedly perform one or only a few tasks.

Let us look at tension at the muscular level. Muscles are fundamentally able to do only two things: tighten and relax. The longer a muscle is relative to its potential length, the more it can tighten. A muscle that is habitually tight, therefore, has lost some of its potential.

There is a major difference between lengthening a muscle and stretching it. In a relaxed muscle the thin filaments are mostly farther from the muscle bundle center than are the thick filaments. When a muscle contracts, the thin filaments move toward the center. In a lengthened muscle the thin filaments release, and there is no felt sense of tension as the muscle sits in the relaxed position. With a stretched muscle there is a feeling of pull or stretching in the muscle. And, in fact, a stretched muscle sends a signal to the nervous system that is answered with a signal to contract. Clearly, to achieve maximum potential, we wish to have lengthened muscles. This is why Feldenkrais practitioners do not think about stretching the muscles but think about releasing the muscular inhibition through the nervous system so that the muscles lengthen.

Habitual tightness compromises our ability to perform. This is not to be confused with the necessary tone to maintain our movement potential. A person without any significant muscular tone is in very bad shape, as he is unable to sit up, much less move. A heuristic example will clarify how habitual tightness reduces our ability to achieve. Suppose that a particular muscular group has the potential of one hundred units of effort. This muscular group must continually exert twenty units to maintain tonus if it is optimally in use. Of course, no one quite gets to optimal. Let us say someone who is well organized uses an additional five units of effort, whereas if she were poorly organized, she would use an additional twenty units of effort. Figure 4.1 depicts the two situations. As you can see, if we are well organized, much more of our potential is available

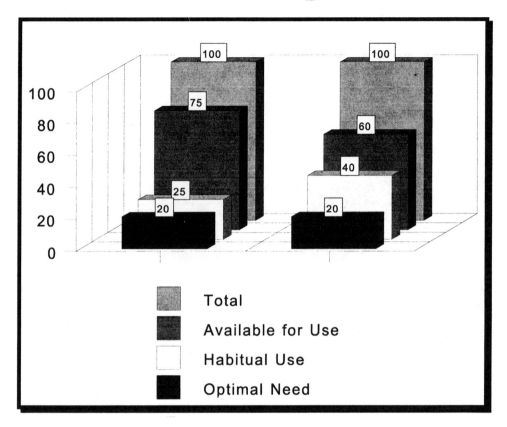

Figure 4.1 Muscular Effort: Well- versus Poorly Organized System

to do what we want. Thus the well-organized individual is using twenty-five units versus forty units for the poorly organized individual. Available potential then is seventy-five units versus sixty units (total potential less what is habitually in use). This means that the well-organized person will be able to perform tasks beyond the capacity of the poorly organized one, unless the poorly organized person pushes past her capacity and risks injury.

Also we can see that any task that is achievable at the two levels of organization is much easier when the person's nervous system is well organized. Thus, if a task required thirty units, it would consume half the available potential in the poorly organized condition but only 40 percent of potential when the person is well organized. Figure 4.2 depicts this comparison.

As the example shows, when we are well organized, more of our potential power is available to do what we want. This makes achieving any task easier and greatly reduces the likelihood of injury.

It might seem from this example that increasing your strength would compensate for poor organization. This is only partially true, for two reasons. First,

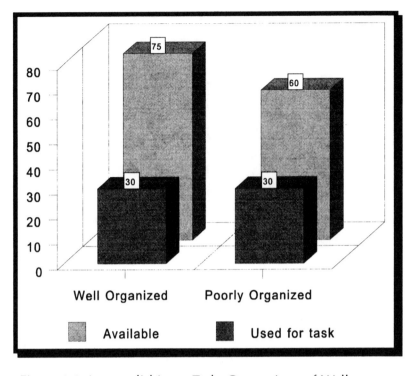

Figure 4.2 Accomplishing a Task: Comparison of Well- versus
Poorly Organized System

you might not increase the strength of the appropriate musculature; and second, there is more to good organization than relaxed muscles. Good organization also involves coordination and proper timing. Thus, historically, when people had heavy tasks to perform, such as shifting rails on a rail bed, they would use songs to ensure both that they would exert themselves on the exhalation and that they would work in unison. By exerting on the exhale, they made optimum use of their strength and leverage.

A well-organized individual, by using so much less effort for maintenance, moves gracefully. In addition, when one is well organized, it seems as though effort is effortless. That is, things happen virtually directly from intention.

REVERSIBILITY PRINCIPLE

One important aspect of good movement and positioning is reversibility. Feldenkrais's martial arts background convinced him of reversibility's importance. Simply put, if you begin a movement and are committed so completely would meet outside their monastery gates and share a smoke. One day they got into a discussion about whether it was appropriate to smoke and pray at the same time. After much going back and forth, they decided to ask their abbots. When they got together the next evening the first monk said that his abbot said it was absolutely not permitted. The second monk was shocked.

"What did you ask your abbot?" he queried.

"Whether it was all right to smoke while praying."

"Ah," said the second monk, "that's the problem. I asked if it was all right to pray while smoking."

There is a major internal difference between singing (where something happens, such as the soft palate lifting) and making something happen while singing. Because of the limited bandwidth of consciousness, we are restricted in what we can control and function best when we can drop control and go into a flow state. Adding any extra layer of controlling behavior increases our effort and reduces the chance of going into flow. It also increases the systemic tension. This is just from the added control aspect. There is additional tension because this controlling makes transitions more difficult. As was mentioned earlier, not only does this controlling behavior make it more difficult to perform our best, but also the attendant unnecessary strain leads to premature deterioration of the voice.

that you cannot do anything but finish it, you make yourself vulneral
surprise. At best, you have to partially undo what you've done, with cc
tant delay; at worst, you lose. For the same reason stances should be syr
cal. If a stance is asymmetrical, the ability to move or resist in at least on
tion is lost. For example, if you stand with the right foot forward, you
move quickly to the left and are unable to resist a forward push from you
rear leftward.

THE WHOLE IS NOT THE SUM OF THE PARTS

A final difficulty brought about from *efforting* shows up only when one (
ers the whole sound or performance. Basically, if you are using extra effc
are in violation of the reversibility principle. You may indeed accomplis.
you intend, but now you are out of position for your next move (or, as a
next sound). An example of this is pursing the lips to make a "fuller" [i]
This may work, but only in one context, that is, by itself. However, whe
try to make another sound immediately afterward, you are out of pc
Specifically, the jaw is pushed forward and is slightly tightened. We perf
this experiment with a student who could get an acceptable [i] sound
pursed lips. However, she was unable to go smoothly to an [e] or a
Basically, she had been caught *out of position*.

Deliberately lifting the soft palate is a common practice. In general
good singers sing, the soft palate is lifted naturally (especially for the
range). But they do not deliberately do this; it happens "naturally" and,
fore, without extra effort. Observing this phenomenon, some teachers cor
ed that teaching a deliberate lifting of the soft palate would be help
singers. However, deliberately lifting the soft palate engages extra muscle
requires more effort than when it spontaneously happens. Thus, usin
reversibility principle, this lifting will compromise the total sound, evel
works in the higher part of the range. The manipulated lifting will inevi
lead to a distortion of some sounds.

One could say, therefore, that for "natural" singers the soft palate is
while singing, whereas those who have learned to deliberately lift the
palate sing while lifting the soft palate. A joke may help clear up what
seem like a semantic distinction.

Two monks, both smokers, lived in adjacent monasteries. Every evening

5

Pelvic Power

THE PELVIS

The pelvis (meaning "basin") is the bony ring of the sacrum, ilium, pubic bone, and ischium (or sit bone). It supports and protects the internal organs. However, its most important mechanical function is supporting the head, upper body, and trunk. Powerful muscles connect the pelvis with these areas.

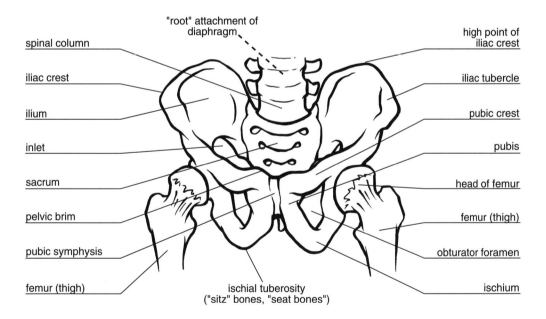

The pelvis or, more correctly, the pelvic girdle (illustrated above), is your power source. It is the location of the most powerful muscles in the human body. It is also the center for movement. The Japanese call this region the *Hara.* They feel it is the key to developing both power in the martial arts and concentration in meditation. A simple experiment will demonstrate this. Lean a little to the left. Did you use your pelvis? That is, did you feel the weight shift from your right to your left sitting bone? Try this movement with just your upper body. Were you able to shift weight as easily? Did you go as far? Or did you have the sense that something central was missing? Another way you can sense the centrality of the pelvis is to stand in a doorway. Now put your buttocks and waist behind you so that you are standing with your rear end in the room behind you. Which room are you really in? If you were to drop straight to the floor, which room would you wind up in? Can you feel that your center is actually in the room behind you? Now that you have felt the central role of the pelvis, it is easy to see its importance. Clearly, then, the more of this power we can use, the better we can project our intent.

VOCAL CONTEXT: POWERING FROM THE POWER BASE

Dr. Blades-Zeller will often ask a student who is just beginning voice study with her to identify where in his body he feels the center of his "vocal energy source." After the inevitable quizzical look, the student may ask for more information. She then has him sing, with the instruction to focus not on the sound (i.e., the product) but only on where is the kinesthetic sense of power source, or the "motor drive" (i.e., the process). Answers range from "the breath," with vague hand motions at somewhere around the midriff area or higher, to "the voice box," with a gesture toward the larynx. She has not yet had a new student who answers "the pelvic girdle" or, by extension, "the legs and feet," but that is, in fact, the answer from a strictly structural standpoint—and, as you will see, also from the standpoint of vocal production.

The skeleton is the structural framework of the body, just as a building's framework consists of steel beams and girders. Like the building, the framework is made structurally sound by a well-engineered foundation. In the human body, that foundation is the pelvis.

Mabel Ellsworth Todd, in her excellent book *The Thinking Body*, explains:

In the human being the pelvis has a threefold function. It must receive from the spinal column the entire weight of the head, shoulders and trunk and transmit it to the legs. It must provide means of motion for the trunk upon the legs, and for the legs upon the trunk. . . . The weight of the head, shoulders and trunk accumulating through the spine and concentrating upon the fifth lumbar, falls upon

the sacrum. . . . The two arches [of the pelvis] are the essential weight-bearing por-
tions of the pelvis, and the sacrum is the keystone for both. . . . The pelvic girdle
is thus made into a continuous ring, so that the body-load as it travels is distributed around the whole circumference. (Todd 1937, 113–15)

Why is it so important to acknowledge the importance of the pelvic center for
singing? It follows most clearly that the spine has its base in the pelvic girdle
and, like a firmly rooted tree, grows up out of the pelvis. The ribs hang off the
spine, much like the branches of a tree hang off its trunk. Effective breath function is completely dependent on freedom of the ribs to expand and contract.
Therefore, if the pelvis is not appropriately aligned and supported, the domino
effect throughout the rest of the system reduces considerably the ability to
achieve full vocal potential.

This has powerful implications for singers who wish to be fully efficient in
their stance, accessing the center of their structural support. Seeing the pelvic
girdle as structural and axial center, it is easy to understand that the legs are
designed to act as columns of support underneath this foundation. There is no
question that the legs and feet must be positioned under the singer so as to
undergird the pelvic center fully and completely. When the system is out of
alignment and out of balance, strain and fatigue result, and vocal production is
severely inhibited.

What about the commonly held beliefs about proper stance for singing that
often admonish the singer to stand with feet "shoulder distance apart"? This is
commonly interpreted as the outer contour of where the arm and shoulder join
(the tailor's shoulder). What does this distance have to do with the pelvic girdle and its support? Nothing, since, according to Todd, "The shoulder girdle
consists of two clavicles and two scapulae, and lies outside the chest, superim-
posed upon the axial skeleton. *It has no direct bony connection with the spine.*" So
when one stands with the feet that wide apart, the pelvic girdle is *less* supported. It is as if a building were supported by columns placed too far apart without any center beam. With the feet too widely separated, the pelvic floor in a
sense buckles downward—and then what becomes of the spine? the ribs? the
breath? the voice?

So where did this idea of placing the feet shoulder distance apart come from?
It came from a *proper* appreciation of human anatomy. If you look at a picture of
a skeleton, you'll see that the hip joints are not in line with the shoulder joints.
Rather, they are somewhat inward. Thus, you want your feet wider than your

hips so that they will provide structural support. However, note that the hip joint is not where the tailor measures your hips; that is *the pelvic crest.* The hip is actually much lower and interior. Likewise, the shoulder width is not what a tailor measures. Lift your right arm in the air. Now extend your left hand from the armpit directly upward to the top of your right shoulder and drop the raised arm. Where does your left hand wind up? It is on the actual tip of the right shoulder. This is about three inches in from where the tailor measures! Standing this wide will put your feet under you in such a way as to provide solid support. In other words, in this position the structural load will be directly down through the bones without any shearing force. Unfortunately, too many teachers and singers look at the outer body and see the shoulders as being the outside of the arm, which is actually about three inches outside the shoulder. This stance is clearly too wide (by about three inches on each side). Standing with your feet this widely spaced pushes the belly forward, which both cuts off breath and requires extra effort to remain erect. The result is a thinner, uglier sound.

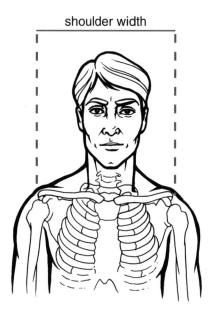

shoulder width

The other "approved" stance is the tripod, with one foot placed ahead of the other. This stance has been handed down from generation to generation. It may appear on the surface to be very stable and strong; indeed for 15 to 25 percent of the population, it is, because these people have either a scoliosis (spinal curvature) or a significant difference in leg lengths (more than one centimeter or three-eighths inch). If you have this structural arrangement, standing with the feet even will put most of the weight onto the short side, thereby compressing the ribs on that side. Moving the long leg forward evens out the weight distribution. But for most people, this position creates an uncomfortable spinal twist and, again, an instability in the pelvic center. And, as stated, pelvic misalignment has profound repercussions throughout the entire postural (and, by association, kinesthetic) system, as well as violating the reversibility principle (see p. 54–55).

Returning to Dr. Blades-Zeller's proverbial new student, once the student has sung and tentatively selected the location of the "energy center," Dr. Blades-Zeller pulls out a picture of the human skeleton. She then asks the student to identify the exact lateral midpoint of the body, just by dividing it into halves between head and base of feet. All students have correctly pointed to the pelvic girdle, even if they do not have the vocabulary to name it (or are too inhibited by social mores to do so!). From that point on, it is very easy to explain the importance and function of the pelvic girdle, its relation to the rest of the skeleton, and, most significant, its critical participation in efficient breath for singing. When she has the student sing again, she asks him to attend only to the kinesthetic sense of power and center deriving from the pelvis. The results are consistently apparent, both to the listener and to the singer: a freer, fuller, easier, and more responsive singing voice pours forth. This initial empirical understanding and kinesthetic experience become the basis for all their work from then on.

The following lesson will help you get you in touch with your pelvis as your power center.

ATM: Pelvic Clock

This lesson may be done lying on the floor or sitting in a chair. To facilitate use in many situations, directions are for using a chair. To convert to a floor lesson, lie with your legs bent and the soles of your feet on the floor when doing the movements and with the legs stretched out when resting or scanning. Occasionally doing the lesson on the floor is recommended, as it is more powerful, and varying position reduces the tendency to become mechanical.

1. Sit in a chair that has a firm, flat bottom. Come forward so that your feet are firmly on the floor. **Tilt your pelvis backward so that your back rounds.** Then return to neutral. Repeat this movement *slowly* 5 or 6 times.

    Now rock your pelvis forward as your back arches. Repeat this movement 5 or 6 times.

    Then combine the two movements. Repeat 4 or 5 times. *It is very important that you use your pelvis to lead this movement.* It is better to make a small movement where you are certain that you are rocking from the pelvis than a large movement where it is unclear that this is the case.

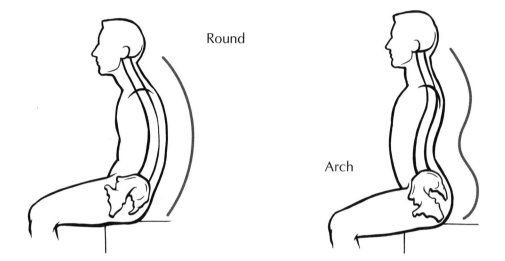

2.   **Lift your right hip slightly.** Repeat 4 or 5 times and then pause.

     Now repeat the movement, but concentrate on putting the weight down through your left hip to raise the right. Pause after another 4 to 5 repetitions.

3.   **Now lift your left hip. Concentrate on putting the weight down through your right hip as you do this.** Repeat 5 or 6 times.

4.   **Alternate between lifting the left and the right hip.** Do this at least 8 times. *Have the sense that your pelvis leads this movement.* Is it easier to move left or right? Does this movement become more even as you repeat it? Pause.

     Round and arch the back. Repeat 3 to 5 times. How has this changed since you did it earlier?

This is the end of this module. If you stop here, pause a moment before standing. Then stand and notice any changes. Finally walk a little and notice if it feels different. Resume at step 5.

5. Sit forward in your chair with your ankles directly under your knees. Imagine that there is a clock on your pelvic region. Six o'clock is about an inch below your navel, and you focus there when your back is arched. Twelve o'clock is above your navel; you focus there when your back is rounded. Three o'clock is off toward the left hip, and nine o'clock off toward the right hip. **Put your clock at twelve o'clock. Now, move from twelve o'clock to three o'clock passing through one o'clock and two o'clock on the way. Then return to twelve o'clock through one o'clock and two o'clock.** *Clearly sense where one and two o'clock are as you make this movement.* Be very clear that you are making a quarter circle. If it does not feel rounded, decrease the size until it does. Repeat this movement at least 7 times. Go slowly enough so that all the hours are clear to you each time you make the movement. Pause.

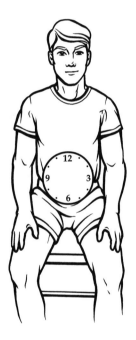

6. **Now go from three o'clock to six o'clock. Pass through four and five on the way.** Repeat this 5 to 7 times, being clear about all the hours.

   Combine this movement with the last one and go from six o'clock to twelve o'clock via one two, three, four, and five. Do this 3 or 4 times and then pause. Rest back in the chair (stretch out your legs if you're on the floor). Compare your left and right sides.

7. **Go from twelve o'clock to eleven o'clock and back. After you've done
    this once, extend to ten o'clock. Continue to add an hour after you've
    gone from twelve and back to twelve until you reach six o'clock. Then
    go back and forth between twelve and six o'clock via seven, eight, nine,
    ten, and eleven.** Do this movement 5 or 6 times. Again be clear that you
    are moving in a circular fashion. Be aware of each hour as you pass
    through it. Pause and compare sides.

8. **Beginning at twelve o'clock make 3 or 4 movements around the clock
    face going clockwise.** Pause. How are you sitting? Stand and sense how
    tall you feel. How well does your back support you? How is your weight
    distributed over your feet?

This is the end of this module. If you stop here, pause a moment before standing.
Then stand and notice any changes. Finally, walk a little and notice whether it
feels different. Resume at step 9.

---

9. **Again make clockwise movements starting at twelve o'clock and going
    around the clock. After you have made 3 of these, reverse direction and
    make 4 counterclockwise.** Which way was easier? How well were you
    able to feel each hour as you passed through it? Pause.

10. **Move clockwise slowly.** Pay attention at each hour. *Where do you feel the
    movement is sticky or not round?* Make a note of these places. Sense which
    place is stickiest and most out of round. Repeat the clockwise movement 3
    times while making these mental notes. Pause.

    Make 3 counterclockwise movements. Again notice where the movement
    is not smooth or circular. Pause.

11. Recall the movements you just did. Think where you had the greatest dif-
    ficulty in making a smooth rounded movement. Place your pelvic clock at
    that time—1:00, 4:20, 9:10, etc. **Now make a movement of one and a half
    hours in either direction from this place.** Thus if your difficult place was
    one o'clock, go from 11:30 to 2:30; if it was 8:30, go from seven to ten

o'clock, and so on. Repeat this movement 4 to 6 times. This is referred to as oiling the clock. Pause and rest for a moment.

12. **Make 3 movements clockwise and then 3 more counterclockwise.** Be aware of where your difficult place is now. What happened to the place you just oiled?

    Wherever you notice the most difficulty now, oil it as you did in the previous instruction. Pause. **Again make 3 movements clockwise and counterclockwise.** Stop. Notice how you are sitting. Sense your back, your breathing, how erect you feel.

This is the end of this module. If you stop here, pause a moment before standing. Then stand and notice any changes. Finally, walk a little and notice whether it feels different. Resume at step 13.

---

13. Sit forward in your chair and be certain that your ankles are lined up below your knees. **Go slowly, and as circularly as you can, make a few movements clockwise and a few counterclockwise.** How is this now? Were you clear as to what hour you were at?

14. **Cross your right foot in front of your left foot on the floor. In this position begin to make clockwise circles. After you have done 3, reverse direction and make 3 more. Uncross your feet and pause. Now cross your left foot in front of your right.**

    Once again make 3 circles in each direction. *Feel whether or not they are circular.* If they are not, adjust your circles so they are. Uncross your feet. Stop and rest a moment.

15. Put the soles of your feet together. **In this position go clockwise around the clock.** Can you stay aware of the hours as you do this? Were there any sticky places? Repeat 3 times. Pause.

    Reverse direction and go counterclockwise. Repeat 3 times. Where did you have the most difficulty doing these movements?

Go to that time and oil the clock as you did earlier. Then go around the clock in each direction once. What was it like? Were the circles rounder?

Make several clocks in each direction without concerning yourself about where the hours are. Stop. Separate your feet and put them both on the floor.

16. **Make 3 clockwise movements. Then reverse direction and make another 3 movements.** How is this different from before you changed the position of your feet? How erect are you? How easy is it to stay seated like this? Notice your breathing, the feeling in your back, the feeling in your hips. Stand up and notice how you feel. Walk around for a minute or two and notice how this feels.

END OF LESSON

There are many possible variants for this lesson. Please do the lesson in the above form at least four times before exploring the variations. You can change the size of your clock for an easy variation. Another variation is to put the soles of your feet together and do this lesson as written either seated or, if lying, either propped up on your elbows or with arms extended. These variations act to open up the hip joints. Or you can focus on the movement of the head. Notice that it also describes a clock with the pelvis. Then have the head lead the movement. If you are brave, you can try having these clocks going in opposition or starting one at six and the other at twelve o'clock. Yet another possibility is to sit with only one buttock on the chair (or, on the floor, one leg up and the other down).

But, please, whatever variation you try, stick with the basic idea of the power coming from the pelvis with the torso on top of it. It is easy to dream up variations that seem plausible but that don't work or that work too poorly to justify the effort.

THE PELVIS IN SITTING

Because it acts both as a basin and as the support for the trunk, the pelvis is critical to sitting erect. Ideally the weight should be evenly distributed on your sitting bones. When it is, you can press straight down through the shoulders without collapsing the back or causing discomfort. The key to this position is having the pelvis underneath the trunk, not too far forward, as in slouching, or too far back, as when hyperextended. Unfortunately, most people never learn to sit up straight.

Slouching is the almost universal teenage posture, at least for North Americans. While this does not cause significant discomfort when you are young, it always impedes vocal output. Slouching, or sitting with a rounded back, involves both compressing the sternum and flattening out the ribs. This reduces the capacity to draw in air. Slouching also constricts the muscles around the throat and pulls the jaw downward. Slouch for a moment, and you will be able to feel these effects. Imagine singing while slouching. Of course, no one actually tries to do so (except for a very small number of roles where this might be effective).

However, if slouching is your habitual posture, it will be difficult to remain fully erect for a long time, as the erect position will require unaccustomed effort. The system is not used to balancing properly and will need to use muscular effort to remain balanced. This need not be. When proper erect posture is the norm, it has that effortless quality of rightness. This is because the weight is carried by the spine with just the minimum effort needed to keep it in balance. In this position, the breathing apparatus is fully available and there is no excess tension in the jaw or throat.

It is possible to be overly erect, or hyperextended. Female gymnasts use hyperextension as part of their technique. When this is the habitual position, there is a rigidity to the system and a tense feeling overall. The shoulder blades are retracted. As a result, breathing is impeded, and a strained quality is imparted to vocal production. For those who habitually hyperextend, the balanced erect posture will feel like slouching. They will feel as if it is too easy and that something is missing.

Because improper support is deeply ingrained, it seems difficult to change. The admonition to "sit up straight" works only for a few minutes. Most people assume, therefore, that learning to sit properly is a long, arduous task. The following lesson demonstrates that this is not so. If you do the entire lesson, you will feel yourself sitting better, more easily, more completely on your sit bones, and more properly erect. Of course, one lesson will not completely or permanently overcome years of habit. It will take numerous repetitions to make the relaxed upright posture your norm.

ATM: THE ROLE OF THE PELVIS IN SITTING ERECT

1.   Sit in a chair with a straight seat, if possible. Do you need to lean against the back of the chair, or can you comfortably sit up straight? Now sit toward the edge of the chair. Put your left hand on your left knee and your right hand on the right side of the chair seat behind you. **Move your left knee forward a little and then back to neutral.** (*The movement happens from the hip.* Can you feel this?) Do this *slowly* 6 to 8 times. **Allow the head and eyes to be moved by the movement of the hip and knee.** *Pause for as long between movements as it takes to make 1 movement.* Rest in place for about one minute.

2.   **Move your left knee forward and then stop, turn your eyes and head back to the center, and then bring your knee back to neutral.** Repeat 4 to 6 times and then move back in your chair. Compare how your left and right sides feel. Pause for a minute. Lean back in your chair if you feel the need.

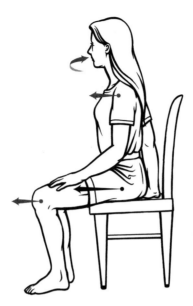

3. Move back to the edge of your chair. Put your right hand on your right knee and your left hand on the side of the chair seat. **Move your right knee forward and back. Allow your head and eyes to move. Notice when you breathe in and when you breathe out as you make this movement.** Repeat 6 to 8 times slowly. Remember to pause between movements. Rest in place.

4. **Move the right knee forward, stop and turn your eyes and head back to the center, and then bring your knee back to neutral.** Do this slowly 5 or 6 times and then move back in your chair. How do you feel now?

This is the end of this module. It is a logical place to stop if you cannot do the lesson in one sitting. Resume at step 5.

---

5. **Review steps 1 and 3 by doing each a couple of times.**

Now put your right hand on your right knee and your left hand on your left knee. **Slowly move one knee forward and then the other.** What happens to the knee you are not moving forward? Repeat this pattern several times, pausing after each sequence to assimilate the effects of the movement. Stop. How are you sitting now?

6.   **Put your right hand on the chair behind you and your left hand on the left knee. Move the left knee forward and leave it there.** The head will be off to the right slightly. Leave it there. **Move your eyes to the center and back several times. Then move everything back to the center.** Do this 3 or 4 times.

      Now move the left knee forward and back several times. How does it feel now?

      Then move the left knee forward once and see how far you can see to the right without any strain. Sit back in your chair, rest, and notice any differences in the left and right sides.

7.   Come forward on your chair and put both hands on both knees. **Move the right knee forward 3 times.**

      Then move the right knee forward, stop, and take only the head to the center and back several times. Pause. **Then move the right knee forward 2 times and note the changes.**

      Finally, alternate moving the left and right knee forward 4 to 6 times. How are you sitting now? Can you feel your sit bones underneath you on the chair? Is sitting straight easier?

This is the end of this module. It is a logical place to stop if you cannot do the lesson in one sitting. Resume at step 8.

---

8.   **Put the left hand on the left knee and the right hand on the right knee; alternate moving the knees forward 3 to 5 times** *slowly.* Notice when you inhale.

      Continue to alternate but fix your eyes on a spot in front of you. Keeping your eyes and head in the center, repeat the movement 4 to 6 times. Now let your head and eyes move with the motion of the knees back and forth several times. How does this feel? Rest back in your chair.

9.   Come forward in your chair. **Put your left hand on your left knee and**

your right hand on the chair behind you. **When your left knee moves forward, look left with your eyes and head and then bring everything back to the center.** Repeat 4 or 5 times.

Then reverse the hands and look right with your head and eyes when your right knee moves forward. Again do this 4 or 5 times.

Now place your hands on their respective knees and alternate moving your knees back and forth several times. Notice differences both between the way you move in one direction and the other and from before. Rest back in your chair.

10. Come forward in your chair. **Put both hands on your knees and alternate moving the knees forward two times. Continue to alternate moving the knees forward, but now when the right knee is forward, look right, and when the left knee is forward, look left.** Repeat 3 to 5 times.

Now go back to letting the head and eyes be moved by the knee movement. Repeat 4 to 6 times. How is this now?

Then move your right knee forward and see how far you can see to the left. Try the same thing with the other side. Finally, pause and notice how erect you feel. Now stand, and notice how this feels. How upright are you standing?

Walk around for a moment or two before going on to another activity.

END OF LESSON

6

Breathing

MECHANICS OF BREATHING

Breathing is critical to life. Stop breathing and you die. Breath also plays a crucial role in being in control. When your breath is not free, there is a restriction that impedes performance. This is true no matter what you do. So why do people often hold their breath in a tense situation? Because it once had biological survival value. When faced with danger, one gathers one's resources by taking a big breath, holding it, and then exploding into action. This phenomenon explains the behavior of lions on the hunt. You would think that they would sneak up quietly and then attack their prey without warning. Yet, when they get close, they often roar. They do this because the prey's first response is to hold its breath and tense for action. This tensing for action allows a more powerful initial movement and greater speed and endurance over the long haul. However, if the lion reaches its prey before the prey can leap, it has a stationary target and a successful hunt. While holding the breath had survival value when humans were hunter-gatherers, this is seldom true today. Rather we need to use all our breath, freely. This facilitates our everyday activities. It also is vital in singing, where certain breath management is needed.

Proper use of the breath is different in singing (and in playing a wind instrument) than in other activities. In most activities we wish to use as much of our lungs for breathing in and out as possible—that is, to use our entire capacity—because we are using the breath to provide power for the activity. When we run, the amount of air we can take in and expel is one of our limits. When we sing, the breath powers the singing. In normal everyday activities the chest will expand and contract; when we sing, we need to keep the chest open and spacious so as not to collapse inward on the supply of breath or hinder its free flow.

The skeleton of the ribs in the illustration below is revealing. It shows that the last two ribs are not attached to the sternum in any way. They are referred to as the floating ribs. Just as thinking of the ribs as a cage can be confining, having a sense of the ribs as mobile is very valuable. Because of both the cartilaginous nature of the connection between the ribs and the sternum and between the ribs and the facets of the thoracic vertebrae and the elastic nature of the intervertebral disks, the ribs are actually quite flexible. They are capable of considerable expansion and deformation. The goal is to expand them properly. For singing, the key to this expansion is what we call "popping the ribs."

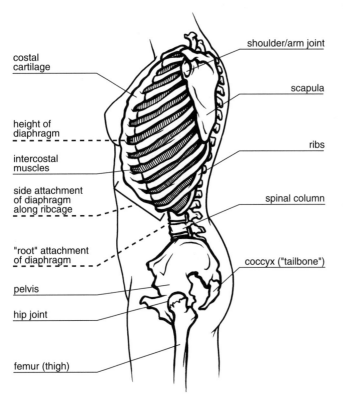

costal cartilage

height of diaphragm

intercostal muscles

side attachment of diaphragm along ribcage

"root" attachment of diaphragm

pelvis

hip joint

femur (thigh)

shoulder/arm joint

scapula

ribs

spinal column

coccyx ("tailbone")

Very simply, the mechanics for breathing involve the following parts: the lungs; the ribs and their intercostal muscles (internal or inner intercostals and external or outer intercostals); and the large, thin, upside-down-bowl diaphragmatic muscle.

When the outer intercostal muscles of the ribs contract, the ribs are expanded; at the same time, the diaphragm contracts downward, flattening slightly. The lungs are attached at the sides to the insides of the ribs and at the bottom to the upper side of the diaphragm. When these partner groups of muscles contract, the action simultaneously expands the lungs both sideways and downward, and a partial vacuum results from the increase in lung volume. Since nature abhors a vacuum and air has weight (14.7 pounds per square inch at sea level), air will rush in to fill the space created. This is inhalation without a sense of effortful "sucking" in of the air.

As noted above, a look at the ribs reveals several important facts: The ribs increase in size (and weight) from top to bottom; the upper ten ranks of ribs are attached to both the spinal vertebrae and the sternum (breastbone). The lower down the spine, the more flexible and expandable the rib. Finally, the bottom two ribs are free floating because they are only attached at the back. They therefore have the most capability for expansion. It is also significant that the rim of the diaphragm is also attached to the twelfth (bottom-most) rib. Therefore, if a singer consciously "asks" (and trains) the entire rib cage to "pop" open, a spontaneous spacious expansion can occur. This action must be coupled with a sense of letting go, or release, of any holding in of the abdominal wall and torso, so that the diaphragm, too, has unrestricted freedom to contract and flatten. What results is a low, nearly effortless, and efficient intake of air that occurs almost instantaneously. The singer feels as if she has done very little and yet has a fine supply of air for whatever phrase she needs to sing. Conversely, when she "tanks up," or tries to get a deep breath, the effect is effortful and restricts vocal freedom. (For a much more detailed description of the anatomy and mechanics of respiration, see Bunch 1993, chap. 3.)

Just as important as how much air we can take in is how freely we do so. If breathing requires a lot of effort, less is available to power the voice, even if we can get a very full breath. Having a free flow, therefore, is very important. This involves using all of the lungs in a free manner. To do so, you must understand that the lungs are merely empty sacs. They open as we use the muscles to create a vacuum. Because this vacuum is three dimensional, the lungs open in six directions: forward where the belly and ribs expand; backward where the spine lengthens, the viscera move backward, and the ribs expand; to the left and to the right where both the ribs and belly expand; up, lifting both the scapula and the clavicle; and down into the pelvic girdle, which moves downward into the hips and also expands outward slightly. Should any of these movements be impeded, there will be a corresponding restriction in the flow of air.

Freedom of the shoulders is vital to the free flow of air. Looking at the illustration on page 74, you will see that the scapula (shoulder blade) sits on top of the upper ribs in the back. If the shoulders are not free, they will directly impede the movement of the ribs backward and up. This will also restrict expansion to the sides, as the upward movement allows more of the torso to expand by lifting the harder portion of the ribs. And the ribs in front also are restricted by the inability to move upward, reducing the capacity of the lungs to open frontally. Therefore, if you are having trouble with your breathing, the quickest and most effective way to address the difficulty is often to free up the shoulders. Clearly this is the case if you feel the shoulders are tight. However, we often are so used to a habitual holding pattern that we may not recognize tightness when it is present. Chapter 8 is about the use of the shoulders. It contains several useful lessons to provide you with more shoulder ease and freedom.

Keeping a relaxed throat and mouth is also important to the free flow of air. There are many things one can do to maintain openness in this area. Chapter 9 has some lessons to provide more freedom in the mouth.

It is very easy to fall into the trap of thinking that there is one right way to breathe. Actually there are many options available for breathing. Only a few of these are effective for singing, and for any singer there will be a best way to breathe at any time. This may vary depending on health. In general the optimal way is the one described above. However, you need to know other ways so that you can overcome problems and can have options in times of trouble. The following lesson is a useful exploration that will help open your breathing apparatus. It employs the right breathing techniques for learning better breathing, but they are not to be construed as the "right" way to breathe.

ATM: BREATHE AND FIND YOUR CENTER

Find a flat chair without arms. This lesson may also be done on the floor starting on your back. Adaptations for that variation will be enclosed in brackets ({}).

1.   Sit forward on the edge of your chair. Breathe normally. **With a normal amount of air intake, expand your chest as you inhale. Allow your exhalation to feel normal.** Try this 6 to 8 times.

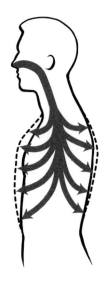

Resume normal breathing. Continue to breathe normally, only now expand your stomach as you inhale. Try this 7 to 9 times. Each time see if you can expand the stomach using less force.

2. **Breathing normally, alternate expanding the chest on one inhalation and the stomach on the next inhalation.** Go back and forth 6 to 8 times. Pause.

    Take in a larger-than-normal breath and hold it. While holding your breath, alternate expanding first the chest and then the stomach. Continue to alternate until you first feel the need to breathe. Then draw a normal breath and let it out. Pause and, again drawing a somewhat larger breath than normal, alternate the expansion of the chest and stomach. Repeat this sequence 6 to 8 times. Does it get easier to alternate expanding the chest and stomach? How many alternations could you do at first? How many the last time you tried? Pause, sit back in your chair and rest.

3. Sit forward on your chair. **Now as you breathe in, expand your chest, and as you breathe out, expand your stomach.** Try breathing in this paradoxical way for 6 to 9 breaths. Do not force or hurry your breathing. Allow the pace of your breathing to be as normal as possible. Pause.

Now alternate expanding the chest and stomach on the same breath, as you did earlier. Do this 3 to 5 times. How is it now? Pause. Notice how you are breathing now. How are you sitting now? Slowly stand and walk around for a minute.

This is the end of this module. It is a logical place to stop if you cannot do all of this lesson at one sitting. Resume at step 4.

---

4.   Sit forward in your chair. **Recall breathing and alternating the expansion of the chest and stomach with each breath.** Do that 3 or 4 times.

Now rotate to your right until your right ribs are against the back of the chair. If you have to, lean a little to do this. {Roll onto your right side.} In this position breathe normally, and alternate expanding your chest and stomach on the same breath, as before. This time, after each breath rest for a breath. Repeat this sequence 3 to 5 times. Pause. Straighten out in the chair. {Roll onto your back.} Sit for a minute and compare your left and right sides.

5.   **Now rotate to your left until your left ribs are against the back of the chair. {Roll onto your left side.} In this position, alternate expanding the chest and stomach on the same breath.** Repeat 3 to 5 times. Then sit in the center. {Roll onto your back.} Compare your two sides now.

Explore the paradoxical breathing done last time by expanding the chest on the inhalation and the stomach on the exhalation 4 to 6 times. Notice what breathing feels like in your chest now. Then sit back in your chair and rest.

6.   **Press yourself against the back of your chair as much as possible without exerting undue force. {Roll onto your stomach.} In this position breathe normally and alternate the expansion of the chest and stomach as you have been doing.** *Again take it easy and slow, alternating a normal breath with one where you alternate expansion.* Do this cycle 4 to 6 times. Pause, and sit forward on your chair. {Roll onto your back.} How does

breathing feel in your chest now? How are you sitting?

Slowly, stand up and walk around. What is the sensation in your feet as you walk?

This is the end of this module. It is a logical place to stop if you cannot do all of this lesson at one sitting. Resume at step 7.

---

7. Press yourself against the back of your chair. {Roll onto your stomach.} **Breathing normally, alternately expand your chest and stomach.** Repeat this 3 to 5 times. Now became aware of the right side of your stomach and the left side of your chest.

   Resume the pattern of normal breathing with alternate expansion of the chest and stomach, but focus your attention on the left side of the chest as you expand the chest and on the right side of your stomach as you expand that region. Repeat this for 5 to 7 breath cycles. Pause, and remain pressed against the chair back while you rest.

8. **Now become aware of the right side of the chest and the left side of the stomach and repeat the breathing expanding pattern, focusing your attention on these areas.** Repeat this 4 to 6 times. Pause, sit comfortably in your chair, and rest. {Roll back on to your back.}

9. Come forward in your chair. **Hug yourself by putting your right hand in your left armpit with your left arm coming underneath the right to put the left hand in the right armpit. In this position alternately expand the chest and stomach while breathing normally.** Do this 4 to 7 times. Pause, take your hands away, and notice how you are breathing now.

10. **Stand up.** Notice how you are contacting the floor with your feet.

    While standing, do the paradoxical breathing, expanding the chest on inhalation and the stomach on exhalation, 4 to 6 times. Notice the contact with the floor as you do this. Stop. Pause a moment and then do the

alternate expansion of the chest and stomach a couple of times. Stop. Notice how you are standing. How are you breathing? Walk around for a moment.

END OF LESSON

RECOVERY FROM ILLNESS

Everyone falls ill at times. Usually it is only a minor cold. However, any respiratory problem can dramatically reduce your ability to sing. Most annoying is the way the difficulties hang on. We seem to have fluid in our sinuses and lungs long after the infection appears to be gone. It would seem that this "crud" is responsible for our difficulty. Yet even when we have cleared our system, the breathing difficulties remain. This is partially because we may not have fully regained our strength. However, another reason that difficulties hang on is the structure of our breathing apparatus.

Our lungs are surrounded by a membrane called the pleura. The pleura adjoins the lungs, then doubles on itself and adjoins the ribs. The space inside the pleura is filled with a highly viscous fluid. This double membrane, plus fluid, means that there is very little friction when the lungs and ribs slide against each other. When there is an infection, areas of the pleura may be inflamed. (A generalized pleural infection is called pleurisy.) Pleural inflammation profoundly retards breathing because it dramatically raises the friction in that area of the lung. This higher friction causes us to need more effort to breathe and also creates some to a great deal of discomfort in that area. The lack of movement in any area causes a pulled feeling.

The following lesson concentrates on lengthening the lungs, thereby freeing up the pleura. As you do the lesson, you will be letting go of places where the lungs and pleura feel stuck. A useful lesson in general, this is extremely helpful for overcoming the pulled or compressed feeling that usually accompanies respiratory difficulties.

ATM: LENGTHENING THE LUNGS

1. Sit in a comfortable chair with your feet parallel to each other on the floor and your arms by your side. (This lesson may also be done lying on your back with your knees bent and your feet on the floor.) Listen to the length of your inhalation and exhalation. Are there places where the movement of your breath is truly clear? Are there places where you feel no movement at all? **Turn your head left and right and then leave it in the center. Gently, with a moderate breath imagine lengthening the right lung.** Fill all the spaces. Notice where this movement is easy and where you might need a large breath later. Actually, "lengthening" is a slight misnomer. You can also feel the lung move to the sides and forward and back. **Continue this exploration for two or three minutes.** Let the right lung elongate in all directions. See if you can feel into some "stuck" places as you proceed. Pause and rest a minute.

2. **Now with a moderate breath imagine lengthening the left lung.** Again see if you can fill all the spaces. **Continue this exploration for two or three minutes.** As you let the left lung expand in all directions, shift your focus from area to area. Notice where you move easily and where it is more difficult. Also notice if some areas are easier to be aware of than others. Is there any relationship between this ease of awareness and the ease of movement? Pause for a moment.

    Turn your head left and right. How is it now?

3. **Alternate sensing the lengthening of the left and the right lung as you draw a moderate breath.** Compare the way the two sides feel. Don't try to change anything; just notice what this is like. **Continue this for 15 to 20 breaths on each side.** This should last two to three minutes. Pause and notice how you feel now.

    Turn your head left and right several times. How is it now?

This is the end of this module. It is a logical place to stop if you cannot do the lesson in one sitting. Resume at step 4.

4.   **Place your left hand over your head onto the right temple. Gently bend
     your head to the left. The left ear will move toward the left shoulder. Do
     not turn your head as you do this. The nose stays pointing forward.**
     Repeat this 3 or 4 times without strain and without trying to see how far
     you can move your head.

     **Now bend your head to the left only so far that you would be comfort-
     able remaining there for a minute or two. In this position, take a mod-
     erate breath and imagine lengthening the right lung. Continue for 8 to
     10 breaths.** This is a little more than a minute. **Return your head to neu-
     tral and put your arm down by your side.** Pause for a moment.

5.   **Place your left hand over your head onto the right temple. Gently bend
     your head to the left only so far that you would be comfortable remain-
     ing there for a minute or two. In this configuration, take a moderate
     breath and imagine lengthening the left lung. Continue for 6 to 8
     breaths. Then return your head to neutral and put your arm down by
     your side.** Pause for a moment. Compare your two sides.

6.   **Place your left hand over your head onto the right temple. Gently bend
     your head to the left only so far that you would be comfortable remain-
     ing there for a minute or two. In this configuration, take a moderate
     breath and imagine lengthening first your right and then your left lung.
     Alternate back and forth 5 or 6 times.** Note whether it is easier to length-
     en the left or the right lung. Which lung do you experience as being more
     complete? **Now return your head to neutral and put your arm down by
     your side.** Pause for a moment.

Turn your head left and right.

7. **Place your right hand over your head onto the left temple. Gently bend your head to the right only so far that you would be comfortable remaining there for a minute or two. In this configuration, take a moderate breath and imagine lengthening the left lung. Continue for 8 to 10 breaths.** Is it easier or more difficult to have your head over to this side? **Now return your head to neutral and put your arm down by your side.** Pause for a moment.

8. **Place your right hand over your head onto the left temple. Gently bend your head to the right only so far that you would be comfortable remaining there for a minute or two. In this configuration, take a moderate breath and imagine lengthening the right lung. Continue for 8 to 10 breaths. Then return your head to neutral and put your arm down by your side.** Pause for a moment.

9. **Place your right hand over your head onto the left temple. Gently bend your head to the right only so far that you would be comfortable remaining there for a minute or two. In this configuration, take a moderate breath and imagine alternately lengthening your left and your right lung. Continue for 8 to 10 breaths. Then return your head to neutral and put your arm down by your side.** Pause for a moment.

10. **Now alternate sensing the lengthening of the left and the right lung as you draw a moderate breath. Take about 6 to 8 breaths on either side.** Compare the way the two sides feel. Don't try to change anything; just notice what this is like.

Turn your head left and right. Pause for a moment.

This is the end of this module. It is a logical place to stop if you cannot do the lesson in one sitting. Resume at step 11.

---

11. **Place your right hand over your head onto the left temple. Gently bend your head to the right only so far that you would be comfortable**

remaining there for a minute or two. **Remaining in this position, lift your pelvis and shift it to the right about an inch.** This increases the sense that the right side is curved. **In this configuration, take a moderate breath and lengthen the left lung.** Repeat this 2 or 3 times.

Return the pelvis to neutral and lengthen the left lung. Then lift the pelvis and move to the right again; lengthen the left lung. Repeat this sequence 3 or 4 times. **Then return the pelvis and the head to neutral.** Pause and rest a moment.

12. **Place your right hand over your head onto the left temple. Gently bend your head to the right only so far that you would be comfortable remaining there for a minute or two. While remaining in this position, lift your pelvis and shift it to the right about an inch. Now take 2 moderate breaths and lengthen the right lung.** Repeat this 2 times.

Return the pelvis to neutral and lengthen the left lung there. Then lift the pelvis, move to the right again, and lengthen the left lung. Repeat this 3 or 4 times. **Return the pelvis and the head to neutral.** Pause and rest a moment.

13. **Place your right hand over your head onto the left temple. Gently bend your head to the right only so far that you would be comfortable remaining there for a minute or two. While remaining in this position, lift your pelvis and shift it to the right about an inch. Now take a moderate breath and lengthen the right lung. On the next breath lengthen the left lung. Alternate between lengthening the left and the right lung 4 or 5 times. Then return the pelvis and the head to neutral.** Pause and rest a moment.

Turn your head left and right. Compare how your two sides feel now.

14. **Place your left hand over your head onto the right temple. Gently bend your head to the left only so far that you would be comfortable remaining there for a minute or two. While remaining in this position, lift your pelvis and shift it to the left about an inch. Now take 2 moderate breaths and lengthen the right lung.** Repeat this 2 or 3 times.

Return the pelvis to neutral and lengthen the right lung there. Then lift the pelvis, take it to the left again, and lengthen the right lung 2 times. Repeat this sequence 3 times. **Then return the pelvis and the head to neutral.** Pause and rest a moment.

15. **Place your left hand over your head onto the right temple. Gently bend your head to the left only so far that you would be comfortable remaining there for a minute or two. While remaining in this position, lift your pelvis and shift it to the left about an inch. Now take a moderate breath and lengthen the left lung.** Repeat this 2 or 3 times.

    Return the pelvis to neutral and lengthen the left lung there. Then lift the pelvis, take it to the left again, and lengthen the left lung. Repeat this sequence 3 or 4 times. **Then return the pelvis and the head to neutral.** Pause and rest a moment.

16. **Place your left hand over your head onto the right temple. Gently bend your head to the left only so far that you would be comfortable remaining there for a minute or two. While remaining in this position, lift your pelvis and shift it to the left about an inch. Now take a moderate breath and lengthen the left lung. On the next breath lengthen the right lung. Alternate between lengthening the left and the right lung 4 or 5 times. Then return the pelvis and the head to neutral.** Pause and rest a moment. Compare how your two sides feel now.

    Turn your head left and right.

This is the end of this module. It is a logical place to stop if you cannot do the lesson in one sitting. Resume at step 17.

---

17. **Place your right hand over your head onto the left temple. Gently bend your head to the right only so far that you would be comfortable remaining there for a minute or two. While remaining in this position, lift your pelvis and shift it to the left about an inch.** This may feel like you are leaning over. **Now take a moderate breath and lengthen the left lung.** Repeat this 2 or 3 times.

Return the pelvis to neutral and lengthen the left lung twice there. Then lift the pelvis and move to the left again and lengthen the left lung twice. Repeat this 2 or 3 times. **Then return the pelvis and the head to neutral.** Pause and rest a moment.

18. **Place your right hand over your head onto the left temple. Gently bend your head to the right. While remaining in this position, lift your pelvis and shift it to the left about an inch. Now take a moderate breath and lengthen the left lung.** Repeat this 2 or 3 times.

     Return the pelvis to neutral and lengthen the left lung there. Then lift the pelvis, move to the left again, and lengthen the left lung. Repeat this 3 times. **Then return the pelvis and the head to neutral.** Pause and rest a moment.

19. **Place your right hand over your head onto the left temple. Gently bend your head to the right. While remaining in this position, lift your pelvis and shift it to the left about an inch. Now take a moderate breath and lengthen the right lung. On the next breath lengthen the left lung. Alternate between lengthening the left and the right lung 4 or 5 times. Then return the pelvis and the head to neutral.** Pause and rest a moment.

     Turn your head left and right. Compare how your two sides feel now.

20. **Place your left hand over your head onto the right temple. Gently bend your head to the left only so far that you would be comfortable remaining there for a minute or two. While remaining in this position, lift your pelvis and shift it to the right about an inch. Now take a moderate breath and lengthen the right lung.** Repeat this 2 or 3 times.

     Return the pelvis to neutral and lengthen the right lung there. Then lift the pelvis, take it to the left again, and lengthen the right lung. Repeat this sequence 2 or 3 times. **Then return the pelvis and the head to neutral.** Pause and rest a moment.

21. **Place your left hand over your head onto the right temple. Gently bend your head to the left. While remaining in this position, lift your pelvis**

and shift it to the right about an inch. Now take a moderate breath and lengthen the left lung. Repeat this 2 or 3 times.

Return the pelvis to neutral and lengthen the left lung twice there. Then lift the pelvis, take it to the left again, and lengthen the left lung twice. Repeat this sequence 2 times. **Then return the pelvis and the head to neutral.** Pause and rest a moment.

22. Place your left hand over your head onto the right temple. Gently bend your head to the left only so far that you would be comfortable remaining there for a minute or two. While remaining in this position, lift your pelvis and shift it to the right about an inch. Now take a moderate breath and lengthen the left lung. On the next breath lengthen the right lung. Alternate between lengthening the left and the right lung 4 or 5 times. Then return the pelvis and the head to neutral. Pause and rest a moment.

Turn your head left and right. Compare how your two sides feel now.

END OF LESSON

7

Upper Trunk Flexibility

The Upper Trunk

The upper trunk consists, roughly, of the ribs and thoracic spine. This region is intimately involved in breathing. As noted in chapter 6, the ribs must move freely for the lungs to open freely and easily. When the ribs cannot properly contract, the vacuum created in the lungs is reduced. This causes a reduction in the ability to bring in air. The ribs most capable of moving are the floating ribs. Their role in good breathing, especially popping these ribs to open the lower lungs, was also explored in chapter 6.

Tightness in the ribs, which is actually tightness in the intercostal muscles that connect the ribs, may have many causes. These range from a broken rib, to illness, to habitual holding of the breath when concentrating. If you have a broken rib, it should be attended to medically. This will reduce the chance that you will suffer a lung puncture. After that, it is important to maintain as normal a movement of the ribs as possible. This will both speed recovery and make sure it is as complete as possible. Chapter 6 contains a lesson, "Lengthening the Lungs," that can help overcome the effects of illness. Of course, proper rest, diet, and, when necessary, medication are all indicated.

When we encounter a difficult task, we often hold our breath for a moment. Then we jump in. This is proper self-use. A problem arises when this holding becomes habitual, as if life itself is difficult. Just for a moment notice your breathing. Then think of something difficult. How much of a stop did this put to your breathing? If very little, perhaps you didn't think of something truly difficult. So try again with something else that is difficult to do or face. If your breath still changed very little, you may habitually hold your breath.

The following lesson is designed to help free the movement of the ribs. It is one of the few lessons in this book that *must* be done lying down.

ATM: FREEING THE RIBS

1. Lie on your back with both legs stretched out straight. You will need about two feet of clearance in either direction. Notice how your back fits the floor. Take a breath. Notice how you are breathing.

    Bend your right knee and put your right foot on the floor. Put your right hand into your left armpit. Then put your left hand over your right arm and shoulder above the area of the armpit. Do not put your hand up by your neck. Extend your left hand and arm to the right. Your hand comes off your right shoulder as you do this. The right hand can gently pull on the left shoulder blade to facilitate this movement. The head turns to the right as part of the movement. If you can, reach out along the floor with your left arm. Do not strain. Only go a comfortable distance. Repeat this movement, slowly, 6 to 8 times. Always pause for as long as it takes to make the whole movement sequence before beginning the next.

    Pause and remain in this position for a moment.

2. **Reverse the position of your arms. Now once again move off to the right with your left hand and arm. Let them come out of your armpit and slide to the floor. Again the right arm assists by gently pulling on the left shoulder blade, the head turns to the right, and the upper torso rotates.**

Of course, the arm position prevents the left arm from extending as far. So don't aim for distance, aim for the same sense of ease you felt in the prior movement pattern. Repeat 5 to 7 times. Pause.

Uncross your arms and stretch out your right leg. Compare your two sides. Then rest a moment.

3. **Put your left arm into your right armpit and your right arm over it. This is the same position as step 2. Bend your left knee and put your left foot on the floor. Now move your right hand and arm to the left. This time the left hand helps by assisting the right shoulder to move and the head turns to the left.** Repeat this movement 6 to 8 times. See if you can make the movement smoother or easier each time you repeat it.

    Pause and remain in this position for a moment.

4. **Reverse the position of your arms. Once again move off to the left with your right hand and arm. Let the head turn and feel the torso rotate to the right. The right arm assists this movement.** Repeat 5 to 7 times. See if you can make this movement easier than when the right arm is on top. Pause.

    Uncross your arms and stretch out your legs. Compare your two sides. Do they feel more even? How does your back fit the floor now? What is your breathing like? Rest.

This is the end of this module. It is a logical place to stop if you cannot do the lesson in one sitting. Resume at step 5.

---

5. **Bend your left leg and put your left foot on the floor. Put your left hand into your right armpit. Place your right hand over your left arm and shoulder. Fix your eyes on a point on the ceiling. Now move your right hand and arm to the left. This time the left hand helps by assisting the right shoulder to move. Do not allow your head to move.** Repeat this 5 to 7 times. Notice whether or not you hold your breath. See if you can release it or make it easier as you do the movement. Remember to pause between movements for as long as it takes to complete a movement sequence.

Pause for a moment and remain in this position.

6.   **Reverse the position of your arms. Once again move off to the left with your right hand and arm. Again hold your head stable by fixing your eyes on a point on the ceiling.** Repeat 4 to 6 times. Can you make each movement easier, lighter? Pause.

Uncross your arms, stretch out your legs , and rest for a moment.

7.   **Bend your right leg and put your right foot on the floor. Put your right hand into your left armpit. Place your left hand over your right arm and shoulder. Fix your eyes on a point on the ceiling. Now move your left hand and arm to the right. This time the right hand helps by assisting the left shoulder to move. Your head stays still.** Repeat 6 to 8 times. Is this easier or more difficult then going to the left? How does the movement change as you repeat it?

Pause for a moment and remain in this position.

8.   **Reverse the position of your arms. Keeping your head stable by fixing your eyes on a point on the ceiling, move your left hand and arm to the right.** Repeat 5 to 7 times. Can you smile as you make this movement?

Uncross your arms, stretch out your legs, and rest for a moment. Compare your two sides. How does your back fit the floor now? What is your breathing like? Rest.

This is the end of this module. It is a logical place to stop if you cannot do the lesson in one sitting. Resume at step 9.

---

9.   **Bend your right leg and put your right foot on the floor. Put your right hand into your left armpit. Place your left hand over your right arm and shoulder. Now move your left hand and arm to the right. This time the right hand helps by assisting the left shoulder to move. At the same time, your head turns to the left.** Repeat this 6 to 8 times. Go slowly so that

the movement of head and arm is simultaneous. Smile occasionally to ensure you are not using too much effort.

Pause for a moment and remain in this position.

10. **Reverse the position of your arms. Again move your head to the left as you move your torso and left arm to the right.** Repeat this 5 to 7 times. See if you can make each movement a little clearer. Pause.

Uncross your arms, stretch out your legs, and rest for a moment.

11. **Bend your left leg and put your left foot on the floor. Put your left hand into your right armpit. Place your right hand over your left arm and shoulder. Move your right hand and arm to the left. At the same time, move your head to the right.** Repeat this 5 to 7 times. How does your head turn in this direction compared to going left? Are you trying to go as far with your arm as earlier? Or are you content to go only as far as you can easily?

Pause for a moment in this position.

12. **Reverse the position of your arms. Now move your torso and right arm to the left as you move your head to the right.** Repeat this 4 to 6 times. How do you breathe as you do this movement? Are you inhaling and exhaling in a pattern? Just be aware of what you are doing. Pause.

Uncross your arms, stretch out your legs, and rest for a moment. Compare your two sides. How does your back fit the floor now? What is your breathing like? Rest.

This is the end of this module. It is a logical place to stop if you cannot do the lesson in one sitting. Resume at step 13.

---

13. **Bend both your knees and put both your feet on the floor. Cross your arms with one going into the armpit and the other on top in the way you**

prefer. **Now move your right hand and arm to the left. The left hand helps by assisting the right shoulder to move and the head turns to the left. When you return to the center, continue over to the right. The right hand now assists the right arm and the head turns to the right as well.** Repeat this sequence of going left and right 5 to 7 times. Pause after every other sequence for as long as one back and forth takes. Allow the movement to be pleasurable and light.

Pause for a moment in this position.

14. **Reverse your arms. Start the movement in the direction you prefer and then go the other direction.** Repeat this sequence 4 to 6 times.

Pause for a moment in this position.

15. **Again start the movement of your arms in the direction you prefer, but have your head go the opposite direction. This means it moves toward the rising shoulder.** Repeat this sequence 4 to 6 times. Can you keep the movement light? Did you remember to pause every other movement for a while? Pause.

Reverse the position of your arms and resume the movement. Repeat this sequence 4 to 6 times. Do you find your feet and buttocks moving relative to each other? If so, this may be reversed by having the head move in the same direction as the leading arm.

Pause and remain in this position.

16. **Play with first having the head go with, and then opposite to, the arms and torso. Switch the arms as you do this. Do as many or few repetitions as you feel like.** Play with the length or absence of pauses between repetitions. Stop when you are satisfied.

Uncross your arms, stretch out your legs, and rest for a moment. Compare your two sides. How does your back fit the floor now? What is your breathing like? How free do your ribs feel? How long does your back feel? Rest a moment.

Slowly sit up. Stay seated a moment and then come to standing. Stand for a moment and notice what this feels like. Then walk around and notice how this feels.

END OF LESSON

THE MIDSPINE

Each of the ribs is attached to the spine. There are facets on both sides of the vertebrae where the ribs (actually cartilaginous connecting tissue) attach. Because of this close connection, any difficulty in moving the spine will impede movement of the ribs and hence breathing.

The spine moves in three planes. It can move up and down, left and right, and forward and back. By combining these, the spine is also capable of rotation. Thus you can twist to your right to look behind yourself. Various areas of the spine can move more or less. However, the key to good movement is for the entire spine, from the neck to the pelvis, to move in unison. A stuck place anywhere leads first to difficulty and ultimately to discomfort and pain, although usually the pain is not where we are stuck. Instead the pain is usually where there is extra movement or effort to compensate. Of course, we can only hope to approximate even and appropriate movement. And it is easy to be deceived by how well one moves when young, because we can move one area of the spine excessively to substitute for a tightness elsewhere. Although the spine can be said to move in three planes—back and forth, left and right, and up and down—in actual movement, it moves some in at least two and usually all three directions at once. Thus, movement forward or back inevitably involves some up-and-down movement, and so on.

The lessons in chapter 5 as well as the first lesson in chapter 9 explore the up-and-down and forward-and-back movement of the spine. The first lesson in this chapter involves rotation of the spine. The following lesson is about moving the spine left and right. As you become familiar with it, you may look at how your movement deviates from this plane and includes some forward-and-back, or up-and-down, or rotational movement as well. If you find that the movement left is significantly different from that to the right, you may have a scoliosis, or curvature of the spine.

ATM: Lateral Flexion

1.   Sit forward in your chair. **Without bending forward, move your right arm toward the floor by bending sideways.** Notice how far you went and how easy this was to do.

      Now do the same movement to the left. Which hand was closer to the floor? Was it easy or more difficult to do the movement in this direction? Pause.

2.   **Tilt your head to the right. Do this *without* turning the head. That is, the nose faces forward and your right ear moves toward your shoulder.** Repeat this 4 to 7 times. See how gently you can do this movement. Let your breath out as you move your head downward to the right. Does this help the movement? Pause

3. **Tilt your head to the left. Again the nose faces forward.** Repeat this 4 to 7 times. How is the movement on this side different from that on the right? What are you doing with your pelvis when you do this movement? Pause.

4. **Tilt your head once to the left and then once to the right,** *slowly.* Repeat this 4 to 7 times. Notice differences between the two sides. Do you remember to exhale as the head goes to the side? What other movement do you notice in conjunction with the movement of the head? Pause.

   Do the first movement. That is, alternately move the right arm and then the left arm toward the floor. Notice if anything has changed. If you notice changes, repeat the motion 2 or 3 times and see if you can notice any other changes. Pause.

This is the end of this module. It is a logical place to stop if you cannot do the lesson in one sitting. Resume at step 5.

---

5. **Gently move the right hip toward the right shoulder, slightly. Keep this a very small movement. The buttock need not lift from the chair.** Repeat this movement 4 or 5 times. As you do so, see what happens if you put weight down through the left buttock to help raise the right hip. Does it make this movement easier?

   Continue this movement, and at the same time tilt the right ear toward the right shoulder. Repeat 4 to 7 times. Pause. Did you put the weight down to the left buttock as you did in the last movement? Compare your two sides. Is there a difference in your breathing?

6. **Gently move the left hip toward the left shoulder. Remember to keep this movement small.** Repeat this movement 4 to 6 times. Did you put weight down through the right buttock to help make this movement?

   Continue this movement, at the same time tilting the left ear to the left shoulder. Repeat 4 to 7 times. Pause. Compare your two sides. Rest a moment. Sit back in your chair if you need to.

7.   **Move forward in your chair. Alternately move the left hip toward the left shoulder and the right hip toward the right shoulder. Keep the movements small and aim for equal effort on each side, not equal distance.** Repeat 5 to 8 times, *slowly.* Pause.

8.   **Now alternate between moving the left ear toward the left shoulder while you move the left hip toward that shoulder and moving the right ear toward the right shoulder while you move the right hip toward the right shoulder.** Repeat this 5 to 8 times. Again, equality of effort is what counts. If you can stay in your comfort zone and do each side well, they will both improve. Usually the improvement will be greater on the side that moves less well. Thus, if you do not strive for evenness of result, you will get it—a paradox of performance that occurs repeatedly. Pause.

     Put your arms down by your sides. Move your right arm toward the floor as in step 1. Then do the same thing to the left. Compare this with how you did at the end of the last module. Breathe in and notice how you are breathing.

This is the end of this module. It is a logical place to stop if you cannot do the lesson in one sitting. Resume at step 9.

---

9.   **Put your right hand on the right side of your face, as if you had a toothache. Tilt your head to the left using your right arm. Keep your neck soft.** Repeat 3 to 5 times. Pause.

     Now put your left hand on your face as if you had a toothache. Tilt your head to the right using your left arm. Repeat 3 to 5 times. Rest for a moment.

10. **Put your left hand on your left knee. Move your hand down toward the floor along your leg. If you reach the floor and can comfortably extend further, do so. When you have gone to your comfortable limit, pause to take a breath and then come up to neutral.** Repeat 4 to 6 times. Pause and compare your left and right sides.

11. **Put your right hand on your right knee. Move your hand down toward the floor along your leg. When you reach your limit of comfort, pause to take a breath and then slowly come up to neutral.** Repeat 4 to 6 times. Pause; notice how erect you feel, and rest a moment.

12. **Put your right hand on your right knee and your left hand on your left knee. Move both hands down toward the floor until you reach your comfortable maximum. Pause, take a breath, and come up to neutral.** Repeat 3 or 4 times.

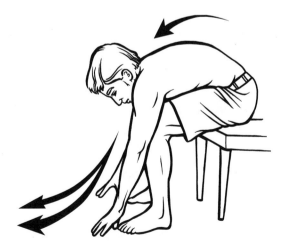

The next time you are down, stay there and move your torso left and

right. This will move your hands left and right along the floor. Repeat this left and right movement 4 to 6 times before returning to sitting. Rest for a moment.

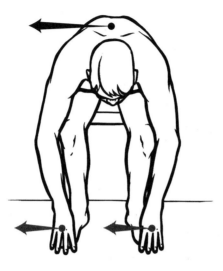

Now, move your right hand toward the floor, along your leg, as far as it goes, once. Then do the same thing with the left hand. Rest. How far did you go this time? How has it changed from the beginning of the lesson? What is your breathing like now?

This is the end of this module. It is a logical place to stop if you cannot do the lesson in one sitting. Resume at step 13.

---

13. **Interlace your fingers and place them on top of your head, with your elbows out to the side. Move your right elbow downward to the right.** Of course, your head and left elbow will have to move when you do this. Repeat this movement 4 to 7 times. See how gently you can make this movement.

Pause a moment with your hands in this position. Resume the movement to the right, but as you do so, turn your head to look at the left elbow. Repeat this 4 to 7 times. Put your hands down, unfold them, pause, and rest. Compare your two sides.

14. **Interlace your fingers the nonhabitual way. This means to look at the top finger and switch it with the next one and so on down the line. Thus if the fingers of your right hand are usually above the corresponding finger of the left, now they will be the other way around. Now put your hands on top of your head. Move your left elbow downward to the left.** Repeat this movement 4 to 7 times. Do not strain to make this side work the way the other does. Just find out, in a gentle way, how you make this movement.

    Continue the movement, only turn your head to look up at the right elbow. Repeat 4 to 7 times. Put your hands down, unfold them, and rest.

15. **Interlace your fingers and put them on top of your head. Alternately move your elbows to the left and down, and to the right and down.** Repeat to each side 4 to 7 times.

    Continue the movement, but also turn your head to look at the elbow that rises toward the ceiling. Repeat 3 to 5 times and pause in place for a moment.

    Resume the motion, only now look once at the elbow that rises and once at the elbow that is moving toward the floor. Repeat in each direction 3 to 5 times. Put your hands down, unfold them, and rest for a moment.

16. **Now take your right hand toward the floor as far as it goes, once. Then do the same thing with the left hand.** Rest. How far did you go this time?

What is your breathing like now? Do you notice any other changes since you began this lesson, or module? Sit for a moment and notice any changes. Slowly stand and walk for a minute.

END OF LESSON

SCOLIOSIS

Scoliosis is a deviation left or right in the curvature of the spine. Virtually everyone has some scoliosis, but for the vast majority it is so slight as to be unmeasurable. The cause for this slight scoliosis is hand dominance. All humans have a dominant hand, even those who are ambidextrous. This is because perfect ambidexterity, where there is no preferred hand, is dysfunctional. If you have no automatic preference, you have to think about which hand to start with whenever you initiate an action. In today's cultures, this would make you somewhat uncoordinated. In less civilized times, the delay in moving could be fatal. The lion or opposing swordsman would slay you before you moved. Thus, even people who are considered ambidextrous have hand preferences. These preferences simply differ from one task to another. This hand dominance means that there will be differential mechanical stress placed on the spine from the two arms. This accounts for the "normal" scoliosis of most people.

Some people have measurable scoliosis. It is not entirely clear why. What is important is that it may affect their ability to function. Typically scoliosis increases with age. This increase is due both to the strain from hand dominance and to the dynamics of fighting gravity when one is off center. For some people the scoliosis can become so large that it threatens mobility and even health. A surgically inserted rod is used to stabilize the spine in these cases. But for most people with notable scoliosis, pain is the problem.

Functionally, scoliosis impinges on the lung on one side and also acts like a short leg. (See the discussion of leg-length differential in chapter 3.) There are lessons to help cope with problems caused by scoliosis. These lessons will allow individuals with slight scoliosis to function, at least for a time, as if there were no scoliosis. Lessons that in large part involve spinal rotation are helpful. The first lesson in this chapter is in that category. The second type of lesson involves feeling the differences in pelvic movement. The following minilesson belongs to this category. It can also be helpful for people with minor leg-length differentials.

MINI-ATM: EVENING THE SIDES

1. **Stand and notice how even your two sides feel. Take off your shoes and lie on your back. Extend both your legs.** Notice how your back fits the floor. How even do your two sides feel? Which side feels longer? Is that the side that feels freer? **Extend the heel on the side that feels freer away from your head. This is not a movement of the ankle but of the hip. So be clear that the whole leg is involved in this movement.** Can you feel the pelvis titling in this direction? If not, you are not involving the hip. Repeat this movement 5 to 7 times. Go slowly and gently as you do this.

   Pause for a moment. Compare how your two sides feel now.

2. **Now extend your other heel. Again move from the hip so that the pelvis shifts in this direction.** Repeat 6 to 8 times. Pause between repetitions for as long as it takes to slowly make this movement. Aim to do the movement as easily as on the other side. If this means a smaller movement, so be it. If this movement is difficult, you can assist by pulling up the other hip.

   Pause for a moment. Compare how your two sides feel now.

3. **Alternate extending your heels.** Can you feel how one hip goes up as the other extends? Can you use this to even out the effort on the two sides? Repeat this movement 6 to 8 times.

   Pause for a moment. Then alternate extending your heels a couple of more times. Did the feeling change while you paused?

   Stop. Compare how your two sides feel now. Notice how you are breathing on each side. Slowly sit up. Sit for a moment and notice any changes in sitting. Slowly stand and compare how your two sides feel in standing now. Then walk for a minute and notice what this feels like.

END OF LESSON

8

Shoulder Girdle and Arms

SHOULDERS AND BREATH

The shoulders play an important role in breathing. Referring to the illustration below, you can see that the shoulder blade (scapula) sits directly over the ribs. Free movement of the shoulder blade is vital to free breathing. Any tightness in the muscles holding the shoulder blade will impede rib movement and thus breathing.

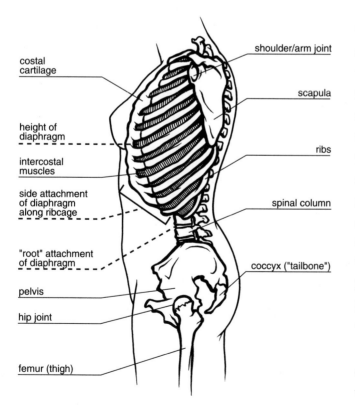

costal
cartilage

shoulder/arm joint

scapula

height of
diaphragm

intercostal
muscles

ribs

side attachment
of diaphragm
along ribcage

spinal column

"root" attachment
of diaphragm

coccyx ("tailbone")

pelvis

hip joint

femur (thigh)

Much of the musculature of the shoulder also overlies the ribs. In particular, the trapezius and rhomboids, the serratus anterior and latissimus dorsi in back, and the pectoralis muscles in front connect the scapula to the ribs. Clearly tightness or dysfunction in these areas will impede breathing. This musculature was heavily involved in the lesson in chapter 7, "Freeing the Ribs."

Because shoulder muscles attach to vertebrae for virtually the entire length of the spine, they are susceptible to being pulled by problems with the back. Think about this interrelatedness for a moment. Can you see why releasing tightness anywhere could have a positive impact everywhere and, conversely, why working one area without addressing other related areas might cause problems? This is the infamous law of unintended consequences. Or, "It's hard to remember the goal was to drain the swamp when you are up to your ears in alligators."

The muscles that attach the shoulder to the neck and arm can cause problems in the muscles that attach the shoulder to the back. Anything that causes strain in these areas disorders the movement or the stability of the shoulder. This disorder is transmitted to all muscles involved in the shoulder, and all shoulder-connected musculature must work to counteract the strain. Accordingly, any lesson involving the shoulder will have a wide-ranging impact. The following lesson, "Reaching Out," involves the relationship of the shoulder to the torso. It therefore can markedly affect breathing and the back, in addition to the shoulders.

ATM: Reaching Out

1. Sit forward in your chair. **Raise your arms in front of you (forward) to shoulder height.** *(Note: In this lesson, "raise your arm" means to raise it forward to shoulder height.)* **Alternately reach forward with your left and your right arm. Repeat this 3 or 4 times.** Notice how far you go with each arm. How easy is your right arm? How easy is your left? How are you breathing? Stop and rest. Please remember to rest a least half a minute when you rest during this lesson.

2. **Raise your right arm. With your arm extended, move your right knee forward, without moving your foot.** The movement comes from the hip. Notice that your arm and shoulder are moved forward as well.

   Lower your arm. Move your right knee forward, being aware of how this carries your right shoulder forward. Repeat this 6 or more times. Each time see if you can increase your awareness of some aspect of the way the right shoulder is carried by this movement. Pause.

   Now make the same movement, but allow your head to turn slightly to the left as you do so. What does this do for the movement of the shoulder?

What does it do for the overall ease of the movement? Repeat 4 or 5 times, endeavoring to make each repetition easier. Pause and rest.

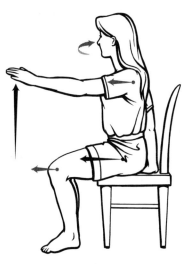

3. **Raise your left arm. With your arm extended, move your left knee forward once, then lower your arm.** Again notice how the arm and shoulder are moved forward.

    With the arm down, move the left knee forward. Notice how this carries your left shoulder forward as well. Repeat 5 or more times. With each repetition, increase your sense of how the back moves the shoulder forward. Pause. Notice how you are sitting.

    Now make the same movement, but allow the head to turn slightly to the right as you do so. Repeat 4 or 5 times. Pause and rest.

4. **Raise both your arms and alternately move them forward twice. Lower them.** Compare how they move now with how they moved when you began.

    Raise them again and alternately move the knees forward, allowing the head to turn slightly in the opposite direction of the advancing knee. Repeat 3 times, lower your arms, and pause.

    Raise your arms and again alternately move them forward twice. How do they move now? How comfortably? How far? Compare with earlier. Pause and rest.

This is the end of this module. It is a logical place to stop if you cannot do the lesson in one sitting. Resume at step 5.

---

5. Notice how you are breathing. **Raise your left arm (forward to shoulder height). Inhale and move your left knee forward. Allow the head to turn to the right as you make this movement.** Repeat 4 or 5 times.

    Now exhale as you move the left arm and knee forward. Repeat 3 or 4 times. Is this easier or more difficult than doing the movement on the inhale?

    Try doing this same movement twice while holding your breath. What does this tell you about breathing and movement of the arm? *Breathing while you work, play, or do any other task is vital. When you hold your breath consistently as you perform any task, you ensure that you will have problems, particularly with the shoulders, elbows, and wrists.* The shoulder blade lies over the upper ribs. Many of the shoulder muscles extend over the ribs. If the breathing is impaired, the movement of the shoulders will be impaired. Likewise, shoulder-related problems will handicap your breathing. (If this applies to you, try one of the breathing lessons in chapter 6 after you finish this lesson.) Pause and rest a moment.

6. **Raise your right arm. Move your right knee forward and allow your head to move.** What did you do with your breathing?

    Continue the movement but inhale as you make it. Repeat 4 times. See if you can integrate the breath a little bit better each time. Pause with your arm up.

    Make the same movement and hold your breath. After you have done this twice, resume inhaling as you move. Repeat the last movement 2 times, then put your arm down and rest.

    Raise your right arm and move the right knee forward as you exhale. Repeat 4 times. Does this impede the movement as much as it did on the left?

Continue the movement, but inhale as you move forward. Repeat 4 times. Notice how much of a difference there is both in the ease of movement and in the range. Pause.

7. **Raise both your arms. Alternately move one knee and then the other forward. Inhale as you move away from the center and exhale as you move toward the center.** Make 5 or 6 movements back and forth like this. Pause and rest with your arms down.

Raise your arms and again alternate moving the knees back and forth. See what happens to the movement if you hold your breath. Repeat 4 or 5 times, breathing when necessary. Rest.

8. **Raise your arms and alternately move one knee and then the other forward.** What are you doing with your breathing? Repeat 4 times.

Lower one arm and move the opposite knee forward. Repeat 4 times and rest. Notice how this is compared to when you began. What are you doing with your breathing?

Now raise the other arm and move the other knee forward several times. Pause and rest. Notice how you feel now. What is your breathing like?

This is the end of this module. It is a logical place to stop if you cannot do the lesson in one sitting. Resume at step 9.

---

9. **Raise your right arm (forward to shoulder height) and move it forward without moving the knee.** Did you move your head? Repeat 4 times without moving the head. Pause with your arm down.

Again raise the right arm and repeat the last movement, but allow your head to turn to the left as you do so. Repeat 4 times, then put your arm down and rest.

10. **Raise your left arm and move it forward without moving the knee.** Did you move your head? Allow it to move, and repeat this movement 5 or 6

times. Each time see if you can allow the movement to be gentler. Pause and rest.

Resume the movement, inhaling first as you extend the arm and the next time as you bring the arm back. Repeat enough times so that it is clear to you which movement facilitates breathing. Pause and rest.

11. **Raise your right arm and move the shoulder back.** Repeat 5 or 6 times, then put your arm down and rest.

Raise your right arm and move the shoulder forward and back. Allow your head to go with this movement. Repeat 4 or 5 times. Pause and rest.

12. **Raise your left arm and move the shoulder back.** Repeat 4 or 5 times, then put your arm down and rest.

Raise your left arm and move the shoulder forward and back. Allow your head to go with this movement. Repeat 4 or 5 times. Put your arm down and rest.

Raise both your arms and alternately extend them. Do this a few times. Pay attention so it is clear to you what has changed from the movements in this module.

This is the end of this module. It is a logical place to stop if you cannot do the lesson in one sitting. Resume at step 13.

---

13. **Raise your right arm (forward to shoulder height). Move it forward with both the knee and the shoulder.** Repeat this combined movement at least 8 times.

Explore the difference between leading with the pelvis and leading with the shoulder as you do this movement. Pause and rest.

14. **Raise your left arm. Move it forward, leading with the pelvis (the knee**

moves forward), then add moving the shoulder. Repeat 4 times. **Then lower your arm.** Pause and rest.

Raise your arm again and now move it forward, leading with the shoulder. Repeat 4 times and pause briefly.

Now move the arm forward, combining leading with the pelvis with leading with the shoulder, aiming to find the most effective way to do this movement. Pause and rest.

15. **Raise your right arm. Move your right knee forward while you take your right shoulder back.** Repeat 3 or 4 times.

Stop at neutral and reverse this. That is, move the right shoulder forward while the left knee goes forward. Repeat 4 or 5 times, then put your arm down and rest.

Raise your right arm and move forward and back from the shoulder while you move in the opposite direction with the knee. Repeat 4 or 5 times, being careful not to strain. Put your arm down and rest.

16. **Raise your left arm. Move your left knee forward while you take your left shoulder back, twice. Then move the right knee forward while you move the left arm forward from the shoulder.** Put your arm down and pause for a few seconds.

Raise your left arm and move the shoulder in opposition to the knee. Repeat 4 times.

Now move the arm with the shoulder and knee together. Repeat 4 or 5 times, noticing the differences. Pause and rest.

17. **Raise the right arm and move it forward with both the shoulder and the knee.** Repeat 3 or 4 times. What is this like now? Put your arm down and pause for a few seconds.

Raise both arms. Alternately move them forward. Repeat several times.

Notice the changes since last time. How much of yourself do you feel is involved in this movement? Put your arms down and rest. Stand up and walk around for a moment. Notice how your arms move now.

END OF LESSON

SHOULDER TENSION

People who carry a lot of tension in their shoulders often complain that it feels as though their shoulder is in their ear. Actually their shoulders are elevated. It may be a habitual response to tension in a person's life to raise the shoulders and locate the tension there. Or it may be a function of the type of work the person does. People who work at their desk writing a lot tend to keep their shoulders elevated. This elevation may persist even when they are no longer working at their desk. Elevated shoulders may also be a response to poor posture. It is as if some people try to hold themselves erect with their shoulders.

Whatever the cause, a high shoulder impedes a singer. Like any other shoulder dysfunction, this will interfere with breathing. It also will constrict the throat and may cause jaw problems. (One of the lessons in chapter 9 explores these relationships in depth.) This particular shoulder difficulty results in tightening of the muscles that connect to the neck and occiput (the back of the skull). This makes it more difficult to keep the throat open, and it may pull on the jaw indirectly. The following lesson is designed to "lower" the shoulder. Please read the directions to the second movement twice before you try it. The movement straight up of the shoulder is easy for some people to confuse with a forward-and-up movement of the arm.

ATM: SHOULDER RELEASE

1. Sit forward in your chair. **Turn your head left and right several times.** Notice how far it goes. How easily does it move? Do you notice any sticky places? Pause.

    Open and close your mouth a couple of times. Again notice how far and how easy this movement is. Pause.

2.   **Hold your right arm with your left hand just above the elbow. Gently raise your right arm and shoulder straight up with your left, until the movement feels sticky or discontinuous in the shoulder.** *The shoulder goes up parallel to the neck, and the arm remains parallel to the torso. This is a small movement, no more than three to four inches.* Repeat this 3 times. Pause and compare the left and right sides.

Let go of the right arm and lift it in the same manner as before, using only the muscles of the right arm. *Let the arm down in a slow relaxed fashion—a controlled letting go.* Repeat 3 times and pause.

3.   **Hold your left arm with your right hand just above the elbow. Gently raise the arm, using your right arm, until the movement feels sticky or discontinuous.** Repeat this 3 times. Again the shoulder is parallel to the torso.

Then let go of the left arm and lift in the same manner, using only the left arm. Repeat 3 times. Pause and compare the two sides.

4.   **Turn your head left and right several times.** How does it move now? Notice what has changed. Did anything stay the same? How far down your back can you feel this movement now?

Open and close your mouth several times. Again check for differences. Pause.

This is the end of this module. It is a logical place to stop if you cannot do the lesson in one sitting. Resume at step 5.

---

5. **Make a fist with your right hand. Slowly raise your right arm (as you did in step 2) until it feels sticky or discontinuous. (From now on, when you lift your arm, this is the point to stop the lifting and begin the letting down.) Gently lower your arm, opening your fist as you do so.** Repeat this 4 times. Pause.

6. **Make a fist with your left hand. Slowly raise your arm (as you did in step 3) and then gently lower it, releasing your fist as you do so.** Repeat 4 times. Pause.

    Turn your head left and right 2 times. What is it like now?

7. **Raise your left arm. As you do so, open your mouth. Close your mouth as you lower your arm.** Repeat 4 times. Pause.

8. **Raise your right arm as you open your mouth. Close your mouth as you lower your right arm.** Repeat 4 times. Pause.

    Turn your head left and right several times. What is this like now?

    Open and close your mouth a few times. What is this like now? Pause.

This is the end of this module. It is a logical place to stop if you cannot do the lesson in one sitting. Resume at step 9.

---

9. **Turn your head to the right about an inch and a half. Rotate your right arm so that the hand faces outward. Now lift your shoulder as you open your jaw. As you drop the arm, let it rotate back to neutral as you close your mouth.** Repeat this 4 times. Allow this to be a very gentle, slow

movement. Take at least as much time in between movements as it takes to do the entire movement sequence. Take this amount of time between movement sequences for all movements in this segment. Pause with your head in the center.

10. **Again, turn your head to the right an inch and a half. Now, rotate your right arm the other way, so the hand faces out. Again lift the shoulders as the jaw opens and rotate back as the jaw closes and the arm drops.** Repeat this 3 times. Pause and compare sides.

11. **Turn your head to the left about an inch and a half. Rotate your left arm so that the hand faces outward. Again lift your shoulder as you open your jaw. As you drop the arm, let it rotate back to neutral, and close your mouth.** Repeat this 4 times. Pause and compare sides.

12. **Again turn your head to the left an inch and a half. Now rotate your left arm the other way, so the hand faces out. Lift the shoulder as the jaw opens, and rotate back as the jaw closes and the arm drops.** Repeat 3 times. **Turn your head left and right several times.** How does it move now? How much of yourself are you aware of moving or responding to this movement?

Open and close your mouth a few times. How is this now? Stop and rest a moment.

Slowly stand up. Walk a little and notice how this feels. Pay particular attention to how your arms move as you walk.

END OF LESSON

9

Head and Neck

POSITIONING THE HEAD

The head contains the mouth, tongue, sinuses, brain, eyes, ears, and nose. It balances on the seven vertebrae of the neck (cervical spine). The neck, which is the top portion of the spine, curves in the same direction as the lumbar spine and the opposite direction of the thoracic spine. At the base of the spine is the pelvis, which, like the head, is relatively heavy. Because of their mass and relative positions, the head and pelvis tend to move in opposition. Move the head forward and the pelvis goes backward, and vice versa.

The neck is relatively delicate compared to the head. The head must balance on the neck. Because of the vital role of the throat and larynx in singing, poor head-neck balance is apt to choke the voice. The head should turn freely up and down and left and right upon the neck. When these movements are restricted in more than a minor way, your sound will be impaired. The lessons in this chapter are designed to provide free and easy movement of the head and neck.

People commonly make poor and injurious use of the head and neck by using the neck muscles to directly lift the head when sitting up from lying. The neck muscles are relatively weak and have little mechanical advantage for lifting the head. As a result, people who habitually lift their head this way eventually wind up with either discomfort or stiffness in the neck. There are better ways both to sit up and to directly lift the head. The preferable way to sit up is to bend your knees, roll to the side, and, without stopping, come up to sitting by moving your head in a semicircular trajectory. This makes use of the momentum of the legs going down to help lift the head. And moving the head and back in a circular manner to sit up both involves more muscles and reduces the peak muscular load compared to the linear movement of coming straight up to sitting.

To safely lift the head directly up from lying, first push down on the sternum (breastbone). This greatly increases leverage over using only the neck muscles to lift the head. It also involves more musculature, thereby reducing the load on the neck muscles. If you want to try this, lie down with your feet on the floor. Then take your hand and push down the lower part of your sternum a couple of times. Can you feel this freeing the neck? After you feel this connection lift your head at the same time as you press down. When this becomes easy press the sternum down without the help of the hand as you lift the head. Can you feel how much easier your head lifts this way? If not, try lifting with just the neck muscles and repeat lifting while pressing down on the sternum for contrast.

Head positioning is a key element in maintaining balance. The head is relatively heavy and is our highest point. Therefore, even relatively small deviance from optimal will impair balance. To find out for yourself, stand up. Then move your head back about one inch, the distance from the tip of your index finger to the first knuckle. You will find yourself tensing up your back and feeling as if you are going to fall over backward. People whose balance is poor often do something very curious with their head. In response to the threat of falling, they look down toward their feet. This better view of the ground gives them a better sense of security, yet at the same time it makes them more likely to fall by tipping the head and torso forward. It is important, therefore, to learn to balance your head properly and also to realize when you are poorly positioned.

The following lesson will clarify the relationship of the head and pelvis. It will also help you position your head more optimally. When you internalize this optimal position, you will know when you are out of position and will have the tools to get back toward optimal.

ATM: RELATING HEAD AND PELVIS

1.   Sit in a chair that has a firm, flat bottom. **Gently tilt your head back (arch your neck) and then lower it so your chin goes toward your sternum (breastbone).** Go only as far as you can comfortably. *Do not force your head back or push to touch your chin to your sternum.* Just allow yourself to feel what your comfortable range is. Repeat this movement 2 times. Pause a moment.

Now begin rocking your pelvis forward and backward so that your back rounds and arches. Do this 3 times. *Be certain that you lead this movement with your pelvis.* Pause and rest for a moment.

2. **Slowly turn your head left and right several times.** How far does it go in each direction? How easy is it to turn your head?

   Raise your right hip slightly. Did you do this by lifting up on the right or putting the weight *down* through your left buttock? **Raise your right hip 2 more times, focusing on putting the weight down through the left buttock.** Pause and rest.

   Now raise the left hip *slightly* 3 times, focusing on putting the weight down through the right buttock. Stop and rest. Notice how you are sitting now. How is your weight distributed? How heavy does your head feel?

3. **Slowly rock your pelvis forward, arching the back as you tilt your head upward.** Repeat this 4 times, pausing after each movement for as long as it takes to make the movement. *Did you lead with your pelvis or your head?*

   Repeat this movement and switch the lead. How did this feel? Can you tell now why it is preferable to lead with the powerful pelvic muscles when there is a choice?

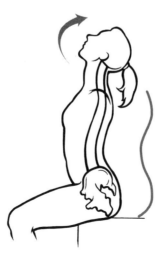

Leading with the pelvis, slowly round your back and look down with your head (round your neck). Repeat this 3 times. Pause for a moment.

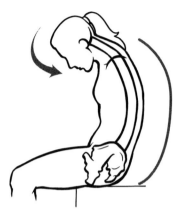

Now combine the two movements so that you rock forward and back with your pelvis as you look up and down. Go slowly and see if you can allow this to be a unified movement where both the head and pelvis move through their range at the same time. Repeat 4 times. Sense how you are sitting now. What are your thought patterns like now?

4.   **Turn your head to the left as you raise your right hip.** Repeat this 4 times, having the sense that the weight goes down through the left hip to lift the right.

      Now turn your head to the right as your left hip rises. What does your chest do as you make this movement? Repeat the movement 4 more times. Pause for a moment.

      Combine these movements so your head goes left and right as the opposite hip rises. Repeat 3 to 5 times until you have a sense that this is smooth and easy. Rest.

      With your head in the center, raise and lower your head and pelvis twice. How does this feel now?

This is the end of this module. It is a logical place to stop if you cannot do all of this lesson at one sitting. Resume at step 5.

---

5. Sit forward and be aware of your breathing. **Arch and round your neck and pelvis, leading with the pelvis.** Notice that you tend to breathe in as the head goes up and out as the head goes down. **Deliberately breathe in as the head goes up and out as it goes down.** Repeat this combination 3 or 4 more times. Pause.

    Now arch and round your neck and pelvis, and notice what you do with your breath as you do so. Pause for a moment.

6. **Once again arch and round your neck and pelvis, but this time as you lower your head, breathe in, and as you raise your head, breathe out.** Repeat this 4 or more times until it begins to feel somewhat natural. Pause.

    Now arch and round your neck and pelvis without deliberately doing anything with your breath. How does this feel compared to when you began? What are you doing with your breathing? Pause for a moment.

7. **Turn your head about two inches to the left. Leaving your head in this position arch and round your neck and pelvis (look up and down using your head and pelvis).** Repeat this 4 or 5 times. Pause.

    Turn your head left and right and compare how far and easily it goes in each direction. Pause.

8. **Turn your head about three inches to the right. Leaving your head in this position, raise and lower your head and pelvis.** Repeat this 4 or 5 times.

    Turn your head left and right. Compare how it goes in each direction now.

    With your head in the center, arch and round your head and pelvis twice. How does this feel now?

This is the end of this module. It is a logical place to stop if you cannot do all of this lesson at one sitting. Resume at step 9.

---

9. **Sit forward in your chair. Simultaneously turn your head about two inches to the left and arch your neck and pelvis.** Repeat this 4 times. Each time see if you can do this in a smoother, more continuous manner. Be as aware and smooth as you return to neutral as when you go upward.

    Now make a similar movement going downward. Repeat this 3 or 4 times, smoothly. Pause.

10. **Turn your head left and right.** How is it? **Simultaneously turn your head about two inches to the right and arch your neck and pelvis.** Repeat this 4 times. Again see if you can find a way to make the movement smoother each time. Pause.

    Now make a similar movement going downward. Repeat this 3 or 4 times, smoothly. Pause.

11. **Look up while turning your head to the right two inches then back through neutral, and then look down while again turning your head to the right two inches.** Repeat this 4 or 5 times, then rest for a moment.

    Now turn your head left and right and compare to earlier.

12. **Look up while turning your head to the left two inches then back through neutral, and then look down while again turning your head to the left two inches.** Is this as smooth as the arc to the right? Repeat 3 or 4 times, pausing after every other arc to avoid a mechanical feeling.

    Again turn your head left and right. Has anything changed since last time?

    Look up and down with the head and pelvis and see what this is like. Pause.

This is the end of this module. It is a logical place to stop if you cannot do all of this lesson at one sitting. Resume at step 13.

---

13. **Look up and down with your head and pelvis.** Did you stay in the range that was easy? How far was this? How much effort did you use?

Now, look up with your head as you round your back. If this is difficult, think of gazing at the stars. Repeat 4 or more times until this feels easy. Pause.

Look down with your head (round your neck) as you arch your back. Repeat 4 times and pause for a moment.

14. **Look up and down with your head as your pelvis moves in opposition. That is, combine the previous two movements.** Repeat this 3 to 4 times. Does it feel more normal?

Now go back to simultaneously looking up and down with the head and pelvis a few more times. What is this like now? Pause.

15. **Look to the right as you lift your right hip (by putting the weight down through the left).** Repeat this 4 to 6 times until it feels very comfortable. Pause.

Now look to the left as your left hip lifts. Repeat 3 or 4 times and pause a moment.

Combine these movements so your head goes to the left as the left hip rises and then to the right as the right hip rises. Repeat 4 times. **Now turn your head left and right and see how far and easily it turns.** Pause and rest a moment.

16. **Round and arch your back.** Compare this with how it was when you began. In particular, how clear is the movement's origin in the pelvis? How well does the movement travel through your spine? Pause a moment.

One last time, arch and round your neck and pelvis. What is this like now? Think of three ways in which this movement feels different. How aware are you of the role of the pelvis in this movement? In sitting erect?

How straight are you sitting now? How free do your head and neck feel? Stand up and pay attention to how tall you are standing and how free your neck feels. Vocalize a little and notice what this is like. Then walk and notice how you feel.

END OF LESSON

ROLE OF THE HEAD IN VOCAL PRODUCTION

Its significance should not be underestimated: the position of the head as it balances on the spine is critical to freedom in vocal production. Familiar signs of mispositioning include having the head stretched up, straining to reach "high" notes; holding the head tilted back with the chin up and out or, the opposite, tilted down with the chin tucked in (to darken or deepen the sound); having the head poking forward like a turtle's or like a horse stretching out its nose for a carrot.

Any of these positions, assumed in order to "reach the notes" or "send the voice out," have the opposite effect: they interfere with the freedom of the larynx to perform the many intricate configurations necessary to complete vocal production.

The impact of interference on the voice can be easily felt. Deliberately lift the whole head up away from the neck. Do you feel the tension that results in the shoulders, neck, throat? Now stick out the chin and feel the restriction in the neck, especially around the larynx and in the cord muscles at the back of the neck. Next, tuck in the chin and feel how tension again restricts the shoulders and neck muscles. Now lock up the jaw and try to talk. Push the lower mandible forward (as if you have a severe underbite) and attempt to speak. Observe the resulting vocal sound and feel the areas that tense. (See chapter 10 for further discussion of the interconnectedness of shoulders, neck, jaw, tongue, and facial muscles.)

Now try these positions while saying, "My head should be balanced freely and easily on the neck, like an upside-down cone on a broom handle." Note the feel and sound of the speaking voice. These positions have the same impact on sung production.

The following lesson relates the jaw, neck, and shoulders. This will clarify why tension in the shoulders makes singing harder. It will also make the neck and jaw connection clear. But, most important, it will help you to free up all three. In the process, your enunciation will be clearer and the ability to project improved.

ATM: Relating Shoulders, Neck, and Jaw

This lesson may be done on the floor or in a chair. The version here is for a chair, to facilitate its use in many places. To do it on the floor, lie with your legs bent when doing the movements and with the legs stretched out when resting.

1. Sit forward in your chair. **Open and close your mouth a couple of times.** Notice how much effort this takes. How comfortable is this?

    Gently move your right shoulder forward and back to the starting point. Repeat this 4 to 6 times. Each time allow yourself to use less effort to make this movement.

    Place your left hand on your forehead and, using the arm itself, begin to move the head to the left about one to two inches. Repeat another 4 to 6 times. Pause.

2. **Again place your left hand on your forehead. Move your head about one to two inches to the left as you move your right shoulder forward.** Repeat 3 or 4 times.

    Continue with this movement, but remove your left hand and allow the impetus for the head movement to be provided by the neck muscles. Repeat this 4 to 6 times. Pause. Compare the way your left and right sides feel. Do you notice any differences?

3. **Gently move your left shoulder forward a little and then back to the starting point.** Repeat this 4 to 6 times. Allow the movement back to the starting point to be very soft, slow, and relaxed. Feel how much of your back is involved in this movement.

Place your right hand on your forehead and, using only the arm, move the head one to two inches to the right and then back again. Repeat 3 to 4 times and then rest.

4. **Place your right hand on your forehead. Move your head about one to two inches to the right, using your arm, as you bring your left shoulder forward.** Repeat this movement 3 or 4 times, continuing as you add the next instruction.

    As you continue the movement, remove your right hand and let the movement of the neck come from the neck and shoulder muscles. Does the head lead the shoulder in doing this movement, or is it the other way around? Repeat 4 or more times until it is clear as to whether you initiate the movement with the neck or shoulder muscles. Rest.

This is the end of this module. It is a logical place to stop if you cannot do the lesson in one sitting. Resume at step 5.

---

5. Sit forward in your chair. **Open and close your mouth slowly and gently several times. Add the movement of the right shoulder forward as you open your mouth; as the shoulder returns to neutral, close your mouth.** Repeat this combination 6 to 8 times. Aim to make this movement more gently each time. Pause.

6. **Place your left hand on your forehead and move your head to the left once. Continue this movement, adding in opening your mouth as you move your head to the left and closing it as the head returns to the center.** Repeat 4 to 6 times. Put your hand down and pause.

    Now combine opening the mouth, turning the head left, and moving the right shoulder forward. Repeat 5 to 7 times. Pause and compare your left and right sides.

7. **Move your left shoulder forward as you open your mouth, and close your mouth as your shoulder returns to neutral.** Repeat 4 to 6 times.

Place your right hand on your forehead and move your head to the right as you open your mouth. Repeat 4 to 7 times until this feels easy and relaxed. Pause and put your hand down.

8. **Now open your mouth as your left shoulder moves forward and you turn your head to the right.** Repeat this movement combination 4 to 6 times. Pause and compare the two sides.

    Move your head to the left as you open your mouth and move your right shoulder forward. Let your head return to the center as your mouth closes and your right shoulder returns to the floor. Then move your head through the center to the right while moving your left shoulder forward and opening your mouth. Return to the neutral position. Repeat this combination 3 or 4 times. Pause and compare the two sides now.

This is the end of this module. It is a logical place to stop if you cannot do the lesson in one sitting. Resume at step 9.

---

9. Sit forward in your chair. **Place your left hand on your forehead and turn your head to the right as you move your right shoulder forward.** Repeat this movement 4 to 6 times.

    Continue this combination, adding in opening your mouth as you move your head toward the center and closing it as you move your head to the right. Repeat at least 5 times until this combination feels comfortable. Remember to reduce the range if it is not comfortable to make this movement. Pause and compare sides.

10. **Put your right hand on your forehead and turn your head to the left as you move your left shoulder forward.** Repeat this movement 4 to 6 times.

    Continue this combination; as you move your head toward the center, open your mouth, and as you move your head to the left, close it. Repeat until this feels comfortable or at least 3 times. Pause.

11. **Turn your head to the left as you open your mouth, and move the right shoulder forward. When you get back to the middle, continue to the right, open the mouth, and move your left shoulder forward.** Repeat 5 to 7 times and then pause.

12. **Move your right shoulder forward several times.** How does it feel now?

    Now move your left shoulder forward and note how it feels. Move your head left and right. Repeat 3 times. How far does it move now? How easily?

    Open and close your mouth several times. How easy is it? Can you feel the connection between the jaw and the shoulders? Pause.

This is the end of this module. It is a logical place to stop if you cannot do the lesson in one sitting. Resume at step 13.

---

13. **Move your right shoulder back a little.** *Do this gently, sensing the connection both to the back and the neck.* Repeat 3 or 4 times.

    Now add in the movement of the head to the right with the right shoulder going back. Repeat 4 times and pause.

14. **Combine opening your mouth with moving the shoulder and head to the right. Close your mouth on the return to the center.** Repeat 4 to 6 times, allowing the movement to soften with each repetition. Pause.

15. **Move your left shoulder back a little.** Repeat 3 or 4 times.

    Now move your head to the left as you move your left shoulder back slightly. Repeat 4 times and pause.

    Finally, open your mouth as you move the left shoulder back and the head to the left. Repeat 4 to 6 times and pause.

16. **Turn your head to the right as you open your mouth and move the left**

shoulder forward. **When you get back to the middle, continue to the left, opening the mouth and moving the left shoulder forward.** Repeat 5 to 7 times and then pause.

17. **Move your right shoulder forward several times.** How does it feel now?

    Now move your left shoulder forward and note how it feels. Move your head left and right. Repeat 3 times. How far does it move now? How easily?

    Open and close your mouth several times. How easy is it? Can you feel the connection between the jaw and the shoulders? Stop. Slowly stand up. Notice how you feel in standing. Walk a little and notice how this feels.

END OF LESSON

HEADACHES

The predominant type of headache is a tension headache. It is caused when tension tightens the neck muscles, restricting the flow of blood to the brain. There are numerous other causes for headaches, the most common of which are sinus problems and eyestrain. If pressing on the sinus areas below the eyes is very painful or if the headache worsens significantly if you look down with your head, it is likely that you have a sinus headache. The most pernicious common headache is the migraine. Migraines can debilitate sufferers for up to several days. Fortunately, most people do not suffer from migraines. Some causes of headaches—stroke, brain aneurysm, tumor—can be life threatening. Therefore, severe headaches that come on suddenly and do not let up or repeated headaches that occur for no clear reason are a medical problem, and you should consult a doctor immediately.

The following minilesson is superb at relieving tension headaches. It may also help a migraine if you can do the lesson before the migraine has progressed to nausea. If you have a sinus headache, the minilesson may actually make it feel worse. The lesson works by showing the nervous system that there is excess tension in the muscles of the back of the neck and occiput. This tension is then released, lengthening the muscles. The release of tension ends the constriction of blood to the brain that is causing the headache. Experience indicates that if you can touch your chin to your sternum, you cannot have a tension headache. And if you do have a tension headache and free the neck enough to touch your chin to your sternum, the headache will disappear. Some people cannot touch their chin to their sternum. Fortunately, that is not a prerequisite for not having a tension headache. Rather, a significant lengthening will result in considerable reduction, if not termination, of the pain. This lesson can also stop headaches as they begin.

Mini-ATM: Releasing the Neck

In doing this lesson, you may find that sequences 1 and 2 are sufficient. If so, then there is no need to continue. Also, if experience shows that the second two sequences, which involve the eyes, work better for you, start with them.

1. **Sit on a flat chair. Move your head to look up and down. Notice how far you can go. Then look up. Stay in this position and open your mouth. You will feel your head go back a little further. Close your mouth while keeping your head in this new position, if you can do so without strain.** Repeat this sequence slowly 3 more times. If your head does not shift position on the repetitions, that is all right. *Do not force any movement!* **Bring your head back to neutral and pause for a minute.**

2. **Look down. Stay in this position, and open and close your mouth. You will likely feel your head drop slightly when your mouth closes. Stay in this new position as you open your mouth again.** Repeat this sequence slowly 2 more times. **Then return your head to neutral and pause a minute.**

3. **Look up. Stay in this position and look down only with your eyes.** Do this lightly so that you do not strain your eyes. **Then look up again with your eyes. Does your head go back a little further? Stay in this new position as you look down with your eyes again.** Repeat this sequence slowly 2 more times. **Then return your head to neutral and pause a minute.**

4. **Look down. Stay in this position and look up only with your eyes. Then look down again with your eyes. Does your head go down more? Stay in**

this new position as you look up with your eyes again. Repeat this sequence slowly 2 more times. **Then return your head to neutral and pause a minute. Look up and down, moving your head.** How much more range do you have now? If you had a headache, what is it like now? Slowly stand and walk around for a minute. Notice how your head moves as you walk.

END OF LESSON

10

Hands and Mouth

RELATIONSHIP OF HANDS AND TONGUE

One of the more surprising close neurological relationships is the one between the tongue and the hands. Dr. Nelson first became aware of this during the third year of his Feldenkrais training. One of his trainers was giving a lesson to another member of the class. She had sat up when all of a sudden her hands locked up. She could not move them; they were extremely tense and uncomfortable.

The trainer said that there was an important connection between the hands and tongue and requested a piece of paper towel. The trainer grabbed the student's tongue using the paper towel. Then he manipulated her tongue very gently. You could see her hands relax. After three or four minutes, her hands had returned to normal. The trainer explained that there were two reasons for this close connection: First, as the fetus develops, the hands and tongue are joined and then bud off from each other. Second, both are highly represented in the sensory system, and these representations are very near each other.

While a relaxation anywhere in the system relaxes it everywhere, as we noted before, the relationship between tongue and hands is a much closer and tighter connection. Very early in our collaboration, Dr. Nelson took advantage of this during a voice lesson with Dr. Blades-Zeller. She noted that there was a great deal of tension and "thickness" in his tongue. Then she watched, with considerable surprise, as Dr. Nelson spent several minutes doing hand manipulations. When he had finished and resumed vocalizing, the tongue tension was gone.

SHOULDERS AND HAND TENSION

The muscles of the hand connect, indirectly but closely, to the shoulder muscles. Tightness in one will inevitably result in tightness in the other. The most common hand-pain problem, carpal tunnel syndrome, is an example of this interrelation. The presenting problem is that the nerve passing through the carpal tunnel is inflamed. Medical doctors will try to reduce the inflammation with drugs or, that failing, use surgery to enlarge the tunnel. The procedure does work, though usually with some reduced mobility in the wrist and a period of considerable discomfort and rehabilitation. However, in the preponderance of cases the problem is not actually in the carpal tunnel but in the shoulder or even the lower back. If the shoulder problem is resolved, the carpal tunnel syndrome usually goes away. The wrist troubles occur because it is possible to overuse the wrist to compensate for weakness or dysfunction in the shoulder. If you pick up a small hammer and make pounding movements, you will realize this. You can make the entire movement with your wrist (note how much this strains the wrist). Or you can make the movement entirely from the shoulder and observe how much wrist strain there is. Or you can try a combination of wrist and shoulder movements.

This is an example of an important movement rule. You want power to come from the largest and best leveraged muscles available, then smaller, more local musculature is available to provide precision. Think for a moment about how this applies to singing.

The following lesson is designed to provide freedom in the hand and wrist. The base lesson can be augmented by the arm variation (variations are at the end of the lesson) if you have difficulty moving the wrist. If you have pain or other wrist problems, *do not do this lesson*. Instead, imagine doing it.

ATM: MAGIC HANDS

This lesson may be done either lying on your back or sitting in a chair. If you lie on your back, it is preferable to have your legs bent with the feet on the floor while performing the movements. When you scan at the end of a module, stretch your legs out. If you are in a chair, sit close enough to a desk or table so that it is comfortable to put either arm on a flat surface. If you must lower your arm to reach this surface, use a book or two to raise the surface to your comfort level.

1. Lie on your back or sit in a chair as described above. Check the position of your feet. Are the ankles underneath the knees (or are your feet on the floor if you are lying down)? **Play with moving the feet to ensure they are comfortable and are supporting you.**

2. **Put your right elbow on the table.** Have your hand and lower arm up toward the ceiling (your arm is bent at the elbow and the lower arm is parallel to the walls). **Softly, slowly bend the wrist a couple of times forward and back.** Notice how far and how easy it is to move the wrist.

    Leaving the hand and wrist where they are in space, move the lower arm forward and back a few times. If you have trouble doing this, hold your hand in place with your left hand. You will feel your wrist move in relation to the movement of the lower arm. *Avoid the temptation to move it directly or to so rigidify the wrist that it prevents moving the arm.* Pause, put your arm down by your side, and compare how the left and right arms feel.

3. Again have your right arm positioned as in step 2. **Curl your fingers in toward your palm. Keeping your fingers curled, slowly bend your wrist forward and back.** Do this 4 or 5 times.

    Now uncurl your fingers and bend your wrist several times. Put your arm down and rest. Compare your left and right sides.

4. Now put your left elbow on the table with the hand up. **Leaving the hand and wrist where they are in space, move the lower arm forward and back**

a few times. How does this wrist move in relation to the movement? Pause and put your arm down by your side.

This is the end of this module. It is a logical place to stop if you cannot do this lesson in one sitting. Resume at step 5.

---

5.   Put your left elbow on the table as in step 4. **Bend the wrist several times. With the fingers curled, bend your wrist forward and back several times. Then uncurl the fingers and bend the wrist.** How does it move now? Pause in this position for a moment.

6.   **Now have the fingers straightened and a little bent back away from the palm. Bend your wrist with the fingers in this position several times. Pause. Relax your fingers, and bend the wrist. Put your arm down.** Rest and compare the way the right and left sides feel.

7.   Place your right elbow on the table as in step 3. **Straighten the fingers and have them bent back a little, away from the palm. Bend your wrist forward and back.** Repeat this 3 or 4 times. Then pause and relax your fingers.

    Again bend the wrist forward and back. Does this differ from the left? Rest a moment.

This is the end of this module. It is the logical place to stop if you cannot do this lesson in one sitting. Resume at step 8.

---

8.   Place both your elbows on the table. **Alternate bending the right wrist and then the left several times.** Notice which is easier. Which has a more connected feeling as you do this? Does this change as you continue the movement?

    Now bend one wrist forward as the other goes back and vice versa. Repeat 5 to 7 times. Put your arms down and rest.

9.   Place your right elbow on the table. **Bend your wrist forward and back several times. Now as you bend your wrist back, curl your fingers into your palm, and as you bend the wrist forward, straighten the fingers.** Repeat this 4 to 6 times.

Pause a moment, then go back to just bending the wrist forward and back. Put your arm down and rest a moment.

10. Now put your left elbow on the table. **Bend your wrist back and forth several times. As you do so, feel the connection of the wrist movement to a slight movement of the shoulder.** What do you feel in your back? Are there any slight changes in the pressure of your body against the chair? Pause.

Now curl your fingers as you bend your wrist back, and straighten them as you come forward. After doing this several times, go back to normal bending. How free is the wrist now? How connected is it?

11. Stand up. How do your arms hang? Walk around for a minute and notice how this feels. Pay particular attention to the feeling in your shoulders and wrists.

END OF LESSON

If the wrist feels sticky, instead of moving from the wrist, include a movement of the arm forward and back underneath the wrist. If this does not make sense to you, begin by holding the hand you are working with in your other hand. This will stabilize the hand, and you can feel the wrist action when the lower arm moves without the hand.

To free the fingers, do similar variations as in the lesson, only with the fingers. That is, move each individual finger naturally, then bent and then straight, and so on. In effect, you can go back and substitute any individual finger for the wrist and repeat the entire lesson.

IMAGINARY WARM-UPS

There are times when you will have to perform with a cold or other impediment. In these situations you have restricted range and resilience. At other times, you may not have sufficient time or space in which to vocalize. It is not necessary to do a full warm-up if you know how to imagine warming up. To use this technique, you will have to work on it some when you are well. This will allow you to feel what your warm-up is like under good conditions. Begin with your usual warm-up for a minute. Then imagine for the next minute or so. Continue in this fashion, paying close attention to what it feels like both to warm up and to imagine warming up. The next day imagine the first and third minutes and actually warm up the second and fourth. Play with this for about a month, doing each imaginary warm-up about once a week. This will give you a good sense of your warm-up. Then practice the technique on occasion to keep it available. When you need to use the technique, do the first minute of your warm-up. Then stop and imagine most of the rest of your warmup. Aim for how it feels when your voice is well. Since you have practiced this, you will know what it feels like. End your warm-up with another minute of actual vocalizing.

THE MOUTH

As with the interrelationship of the head, neck, shoulders, jaw, and tongue, undue tension or inappropriate manipulation with the muscles that circle the mouth can have an adverse effect on vocal freedom. Ideally the voice is powered by the breath; however, too often, the jaw, tongue, and mouth muscles attempt to become agents of "support" for the voice (a role that they should not have to play if the breath is doing its job). The sole vocal function of these organs is for *articulation*. An example of an articulatory muscle impeding vocal freedom is manifested in the quivering jaw, a sure sign of grip culminating in undue tension.

As pointed out in chapter 9, the intricate connection between the muscles of the jaw, lips, and tongue directly affects laryngeal freedom. Observe the interrelationship of the tongue and the larynx: the larynx is suspended from the hyoid bone, rather like a marionette hangs from the hand controls (see illustrations on page 139). The hyoid bone also acts as the floor to which the base of the tongue is rooted. Hence the tongue and the larynx are intimately connected. When the tongue

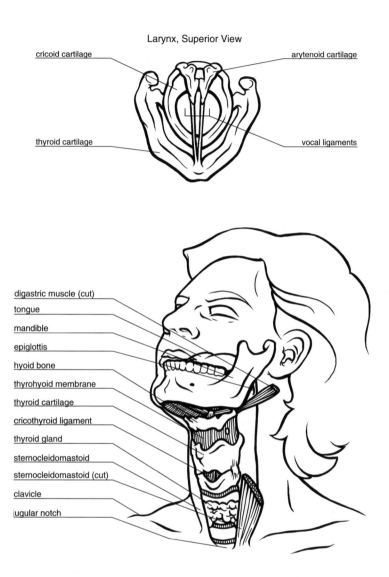

Larynx, Superior View

cricoid cartilage

arytenoid cartilage

thyroid cartilage

vocal ligaments

digastric muscle (cut)
tongue
mandible
epiglottis
hyoid bone
thyrohyoid membrane
thyroid cartilage
cricothyroid ligament
thyroid gland
sternocleidomastoid
sternocleidomastoid (cut)
clavicle
jugular notch

retracts (pulls back)—a common technical fault in singers—it effectively pushes down on the base (the hyoid bone), which, of course, also depresses the larynx, severely limiting its vocal freedom to perform. You can experiment with how this feels. Deliberately pull the tongue back and try to speak. You will sound like either Kermit the Frog or Bullwinkle Moose. Note the tension in the throat and the neck that results.

Likewise, while the connection is not as direct, tension in the lips and cheek muscles can also have adverse effects on vocal sound by restricting laryngeal freedom. Clear vowel and consonant articulation depends upon these muscles along with the tongue. Interference from undue buccal (mouth) manipulation and subsequent tension impedes freedom of articulation and also restricts the larynx. (For more information on this subject, see Nair 1999, chaps. 3 and 4.)

The following lesson will assist you in softening your mouth. As you let go of excess tension, you will find that you can do what you want to do with much greater ease. See if you can retain this sense of ease while singing.

ATM: SOFTENING THE MOUTH

This lesson may be done on the floor or in a chair. The version here is for a chair, to facilitate its use in many places. To do the lesson on the floor, lie with your legs bent and feet on the floor when doing the movements and with the legs stretched out when resting.

1. Move forward to the front of the chair. Have both feet firmly and evenly on the floor. Notice how your face feels. How much tension is there in your neck? How are you breathing? **Now push your lips forward and allow them to come back.** Repeat 15 to 20 times. See if you can reduce your "allowing" effort. Pause briefly.

2. **Push your lips forward and bring them back.** How is this different from allowing the lips to come back? Repeat 8 to 10 times. Pause for a moment.

    Push your lips forward and allow them to come back once or twice. Stop and rest for a minute.

    Sit back in your chair if you feel the need. Notice what has changed.

3. If you sat back in the chair, move forward. **Lift the corners of your lips toward your ears.** This will feel like pulling back and will create a wide "grin." **Then let the lips relax and return to normal.** Repeat 10 to 15 times. See if this can be made to feel easier. Pause a moment.

4. **Pull your lips back and keep them there for a moment. With your right index finger, hold the right corner of your mouth. Then let the left return to neutral. Continue to hold the right corner of your mouth while the left corner of your mouth goes toward the ear and back to neutral.** Repeat 8 to 10 times. Release the right corner of your mouth and pause for a moment. What differences do you notice between your left and right sides?

5. **Pull your lips back and keep them there for a moment. With your left index finger, hold the left corner of your mouth. Then let the right return to neutral. Continue to hold the left corner of your mouth while the right corner goes toward the ear and back to neutral.** Repeat 7 to 9 times. Pause

for a moment after releasing the left corner of your mouth.

Now move both sides toward the ears a couple of times. What changes did you notice? Pause a moment.

Push your lips forward and allow them to come back twice. How is this different from before? Stop and rest a moment.

This is the end of this module. It is a logical place to stop if you cannot do the lesson in one sitting. Resume at step 6.

---

6. **With your *palm facing away from you*, catch your upper lip with the index finger and second finger of your right hand.** The first knuckle is in the middle of the lip. **Gently move your lip up and down several times.** Does it move more easily in one direction than the other? Repeat this 6 or 7 more times.

   Now move your lip left and right. Again see if it moves more easily one way or the other. Does this have anything to do with the hand you are using? Repeat 8 to 10 times. See if you can make the movement more gently each time.

   Then play with your upper lip as the fancy strikes you. Continue this for about half a minute. Pause and rest.

   Push your lips out and allow them to come back twice. What changes do you notice? Pause for a minute. Notice what, if anything, feels different.

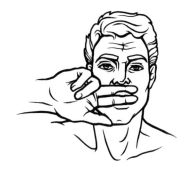

7. **With your thumb on the bottom, catch your lower lip between your thumb and your index finger. Gently move your lip up and down.** Repeat this 7 or 8 times. Pause while holding on to your lip.

   Now move your lip left several times and then right several times. Pause for a moment. **Then resume by going left and right.** Repeat several times. Then pause.

   Finally, play with taking your lower lip up and down, right and left, on diagonals, and in any other direction that appeals to you. Stop, put your hand down, and rest for a minute.

8. **With your thumb and the backs of your index finger and second finger, grasp both your lips.** The index finger will be between the two lips with the first knuckle in the middle of the lips. **Gently move your lips up and down.** Notice where you feel restrictions as you do this. Repeat this 7 or 8 times. Pause while holding on to your lips.

   Move your lips left and right several times. Notice which direction is easier. **Then move your lips only from the center to the easier side 3 or 4 times.** Pause briefly. **Move your lips from the center to the more difficult side several times. Then move your lips left and right 3 or 4 more times.** Pause a moment. Was the movement left and right more even the second time you made it?

   Now move your lips in a circle. Keep doing this for about a minute. What else can you feel moving? Does your head move? How about your ribs? Is there anything happening in the pelvis?

   Reverse the direction and go this way for a little while. What changed when you go in this direction?

   Finally, play with your lips in any way that pleases you for a short time. Stop, take your hand away, and rest.

9. **Go back to pushing out the lips and allowing them to return.** Repeat several times. What is this like now?

Then make the "smiling" movement several times. What is this like?
Stop and rest.

This is the end of this module. It is a logical place to stop if you cannot do the lesson in one sitting. Resume at step 10.

---

10. **Push your lips out, but now purse them. That is, when you bring them back, keep them a little pursed.** This will convert the movement into a sucking movement. If it does not, then convert the movement into what is a sucking movement for you. **Continue to make this sucking movement.** Each time see if you can make it smoother and easier. Repeat about 20 times. Pause and rest a moment.

11. **Turn your head left and right.**

    Resume the sucking motion, but suck only over toward the right. Repeat 8 to 10 times and pause.

    Now suck over toward the left. Repeat 7 or 8 times.

    Alternate sucking left and right. After 3 or 4 repetitions see which direction you like better. Go that way twice, and then resume going left and right another 4 times. Pause and rest.

12. **With your head to the right, resume sucking.** Repeat 8 to 10 times. Do you find yourself sucking slightly off to the right when your head is turned right? Pause and rest.

    Turn your head to the left and suck gently. Repeat 7 or 8 times. Pause.

    Turn your head in the position you prefer and suck off to that side. Repeat 4 or 5 times. Pause.

    Turn your head the other way and suck in that direction 4 or 5 times. Pause.

Suck a few times with your head in the middle. Pause and then turn your head left and right. How well can you turn now? Pause and rest a moment.

13. **Make the smiling movement with your lips 3 or 4 times.** What is it like now? Pause.

Push your lips forward and allow them to return 2 or 3 times. How easy was the return? What do you notice about your mouth? How does your neck feel?

Stand up, sense your balance, and walk around for a minute. Note how you walk and how upright you are standing.

END OF LESSON

11

The Eyes

ROLE OF THE EYES IN MOVEMENT

Like other primates, we humans rely on our eyes as our dominant external sensory system for guiding movement. When we are moving, we want to see where we are going. And when we are stationary, we want to see what is around us and what is moving. This is true even when we have our eyes closed. If you close your eyes and lift your left foot, your eyes will track down and to the left. Wait until you've read the next two sentences to try this. It may be a very small movement in the eyes, so you may need to lift your foot several times to be sure you notice this eye movement. Then if you raise your right leg, the eyes will track right. This happens with no conscious thought or direction on our part. It seems to be hardwired.

The way we use our eyes, however, is learned. A newborn baby has difficulty focusing its eyes. Watching people who are blind is very revealing. People who are blind from birth do not orient using the eyes. They will not necessarily face you to listen to you, nor will they necessarily turn toward the source of a noise. This is primarily because they have never learned to do these things and feel no necessity to do so. They may also move their head in very eccentric patterns when playing or listening to music. Those who have lost their vision, even those who have no eyes, will orient themselves much more like a sighted person. This is because these movement patterns were developed when they were sighted. Once in place, the patterns will, to a great extent, persist, simply because there is no impetus to change and because the eyes also play an important role in balance. Individuals who are blind from birth never develop this aspect of balance. They rely solely on the vestibular system (which is in the ears) and touch. Those who lose their sight, however, have incorporated visual cues into their balance. Even though the eyes are not there, they will move the eye muscles as if they were. Accordingly, eccentric movements of the head will be disconcerting to them.

The role the eyes play in our learning movement is extremely important. It is how we learn to orient in space. Watching a young infant learn to roll over from its back to its front the first time or two is very instructive. Typically, there is no intent to roll. Rather the infant is trying to track something overhead. At a certain point, the turning of the head, which is proportionately much larger in infants than adults, goes past the point of no return, and all of a sudden the baby is over on its belly. One can also watch the extreme frustration when the eyes focus the head in one direction and the baby attempts to go the other way. Thus we learn to lead with our eyes. Indeed, athletes, such as football players, make use of this by watching their opponents' eyes, which can tell them where the ball is going. Or the eyes can be used to mislead, as when a basketball player looks one way while passing another. As command of the eyes develops, we may actively use them to help us learn movement. For example, using a computer keyboard requires knowing what keys are where. Most people have to look at the keyboard as they use it, but with training, you can learn to use the keyboard while keeping your eyes on the screen.

The eyes also play an important role in maintaining balance. The main balance organ is the vestibular system When this system is functioning properly, it is easy to maintain your balance. But if you stand up and close your eyes, you will probably feel minor oscillations forward and back—oscillations that were not present before you closed your eyes. Damage to the vestibular system makes the role of the eyes in balance vital. This can be demonstrated with a balance board, a device consisting of a board on top of five inches of heavy-duty foam. When you stand on the balance board, it is as if the ground sways. After a while, you get your balance and can stand comfortably. However, when you close your eyes, you can really feel yourself sway.

Dr. Nelson once worked with a woman, Alma, who lost the vestibular system in her right ear to surgery for a brain tumor. When Alma stood on the balance board with her eyes open, she did as well as a normal person. However, it was impossible for her to retain her balance when she closed her eyes. Her undamaged left vestibular system was insufficient for her to maintain any sense of balance.

Another way to experience the role vision plays in balance is to walk slowly across an empty space in the dark. Because you know the space is clear, you will not have to worry about bumping into anything. Thus you will become aware that some of the trepidation we feel about walking in the dark comes from feeling slightly unsteady.

Loss of the use of one eye (even if only temporary) requires important reorganization in our movement. A person using only one eye (cyclopean vision) moves the head somewhat toward the other side so that the single eye is more centrally located. There is also more turning of the head and neck to make up for the restricted field of vision. Because the hand and arm on the other side are not seen as well, there is a tendency to use them less than if both eyes were working. A one-eyed individual will also position himself to see other people in a room, taking care to put himself where he can see the most important person(s). When he is with one person, he will try to keep that person on the side of the seeing eye.

RELEASING MINOR NECK CRICKS

We can take advantage of the way we use our eyes to relieve minor neck cricks. As noted earlier, people with cyclopean vision keep the head turned slightly to get that eye into the center of the visual field. This stretches the neck muscles on the side of the good eye and releases the muscles on the opposite side. Typically, a crick in the neck, or minor neck pain, is caused by strained or stretched muscles on that side of the neck. If you notice this happening, close the eye on the side that pains you. If you cannot close only this eye, cover it with a patch. Then walk around for a couple of minutes, if possible. If you cannot walk, look out into the distance as if you were driving a car. Simply closing the eye usually relieves the pain in the neck because when we close just one eye, we turn our head slightly in that direction. This puts our open eye more in the center. This position also reduces the effort of the neck muscles on the side of the closed eye. As these muscles release, the pain slowly goes away.

VISUAL TENSION

Everyone has experienced some visual tension. When mild, it may result in a squint; when severe, a headache. Prolonged visual tension is believed by some to result in myopia (nearsightedness). One source of strain is bright light, particularly from the sun. Unless your eyes are truly relaxed, you will notice that you squint when you encounter bright sunlight. This is uncomfortable, so many people wear sunglasses. Aging can result in eyestrain. As we age, the lens of our eyes hardens. This makes the lens more difficult for the muscles to move. As a result, our ability to accommodate to changes in focal length is drastically reduced; in particular, near vision becomes difficult. Thus people need reading glasses or bifocals, or they will very rapidly feel eyestrain.

Another source of strain is keeping the eyes focused at one distance for too long, particularly if we are focused in close. This is common in our culture, because we spend so much time viewing things at near distances. Until very recently, humans spent much of their time outside looking at the horizon. This involves keeping the head up and open, a good position for singing. In close work we tend to have our head down (reading as you are now is an example) or level (looking at computer monitors). While we can do this, our evolutionary development was rooted in looking out at the horizon for prolonged periods. Curiously, when we are focused out at the horizon, we feel most within ourselves. This a well-known phenomenon among equestrians, who use a technique known as Centered Riding; they refer to this as "soft eyes."

The eyes are a key component of the nervous system. Indeed, we receive about 90 percent of our external sensory input from the eyes. Thus, keeping the eyes relaxed can be expected to relax our entire nervous system. Indeed, when we are visually relaxed, we feel very centered, and all the muscles in the head and jaw relax as well. As a result, the voice is open, clear, flexible, and resonant. The following lesson will allow you to feel what it is like to have relaxed eyes and what it does for your sound and sense of well-being.

ATM: Releasing the Eyes

1. Sit in a chair with a straight seat and no arms. Can you sit straight comfortably without relying on the back rest? (If not, see "The Role of the Pelvis in Sitting Erect," p. 68.) **Now sit toward the edge of your chair. Turn your head left and right.** Did you notice that your eyes move in the same direction at the same time?

    Now turn your head left and right, leading with the movement of the eyes. Repeat this 5 or 6 times. Each time look for any strain in the eyes and eye muscles. Let go of this strain, if you can. Then turn your head left and right 1 more time and see if there is any difference. Rest in place for about one minute.

2. **Look at the wall straight ahead of you. Fix your eyes on a point or picture straight in front of you. Now turn your head to the left about two to three inches. Go slowly.** Turning the head without the eyes is difficult and can be disconcerting. **Repeat this 3 or 4 times.** Each time, go slowly and see if there is any strain in the eyes you can let go of. **Pause for a moment, close your eyes, and put your palms over them.**

   Open your eyes again and fix them on the same point. Now slowly turn your head to the right about two to three inches 4 or 5 times. Pause for a moment, close your eyes, and put your palms over them.

3. **Look at the wall straight ahead of you.** (Read this entire direction first, as it asks you to close your eyes.) **Focus on a point or an image and close your eyes. With your eyes closed, keep this image directly in front of you. Now slowly turn your head to the right about two inches. Keep the image in front of you as you do so. That is, the image moves with you so that your eyes do not move relative to your head. Then return to the center.** Repeat this 3 or 4 times, and pause for as long as it takes to do 2 movements.

   Now do the same thing to the left. Move about two inches and return, keeping the eyes on an image that is moving with you. Repeat this 3 or 4 times, and pause for as long as 2 movements.

   Moving in this same fashion, move your head left and right 3 or 4 times. Pause for 2 movements' time and slowly open your eyes.

4. **Turn your head left and right.** How far did you go? How easy was it? What do you notice about your breathing? Where do you feel your center? Has there been any change in your sense of yourself?

   Now turn your head left and right, leading with the eyes. What changes do you notice? **Sit back in your chair and rest.**

This is the end of this module. It is a logical place to stop if you cannot do the lesson in one sitting. Resume at step 5.

---

5.   **Sit on the edge of your chair. Put your right hand on your right knee. Move your right knee forward without moving your foot. Allow the head and eyes to turn with this movement. Repeat 3 or 4 times and then put your right hand by your side.** Pause and notice any differences.

       Now put your left hand on your left knee and move your knee forward. Again let the head and eyes move with the movement of the knee. Do you feel any up-and-down movement? Repeat 3 or 4 more times and see if you feel any up-and-down movement. Pause and rest for a moment.

6.   **Put your left hand on your left knee and your right hand on your right knee and slowly move first the left and then the right knee forward. Repeat this 5 or 6 times.** Notice any differences between the way you go to the left and to the right. Does being aware of these differences, no matter how slight, change anything? **Stop and rest for a moment.**

7.   Read this entire direction before you begin it. **Close your eyes. Slowly move your right knee forward about one or two inches. Let your eyes move with the head and knee. Return the knee to the starting point and repeat 3 or 4 times.** Pause with your eyes closed for 2 cycles of movement.

       Now slowly move your left knee forward about one or two inches. Do this pattern 3 or 4 times. **Pause, keeping your eyes closed for 2 cycles of movement.**

       Finally, alternate moving the left and right knee forward 3 or 4 times. Stop and rest, keeping your eyes closed for about a minute. Then open your eyes. Notice how you are breathing now. Where do you sense your center? What is the quality of noise you perceive?

8.   **Once again alternately move your knees forward 3 or 4 times.** How easy is this now? How do you feel your eyes moving? What else do you notice?

Sit back in your chair and rest awhile.

This is the end of this module. It is a logical place to stop if you cannot do the lesson in one sitting. Resume at step 9.

---

9. **Sit forward on your chair. Put your hand (whichever hand you prefer) in front of you about one foot from your face with the palm toward your face. Move your hand toward your face and then away. At some point as you move away from your face, turn your hand so your palm faces outward.** You will sense where a good place to turn is for you. **Repeat this movement 3 or 4 times, following it with your eyes.** Perform the movement gracefully, like a Balinese dancer. **Put your hand down and pause for a moment.**

10. Read steps 10 and 11 before you do them. **Again place your hand a foot from your face, palm inward. Close your eyes. Move your hand slowly toward your face. Then slowly move it away. Feel where you want to turn your hand to get more complete extension of the arm. Turn your hand at that place. Then bring your hand toward your face, turning at the appropriate place. Follow this movement with your (closed) eyes.** Repeat 5 or 6 times. Go slowly, gently, and with a sense of grace. **Pause with your hand about a foot from your face.**

11. **Continue to follow the movement with your closed eyes. Now move**

your hand about a foot to the outside and back to the middle. Slowly and
gently repeat this 4 or 5 times.

**Then carefully cross your midline and move your hand about a foot in
the other direction 4 or 5 times. Finally, move your hand left and right
alternately 4 or 5 times.** All the time follow the hand with your eyes. Pause
for a minute.

**If your eyes feel tired, put your palms over them. Softly open your
eyes.**

12.   **Raise your hand and follow it once or twice as it moves away from and
toward your face. Turn your head left and right.** Notice how you move.
Where do you feel your center? How alert are you? How tense do you feel?
What is your breathing like? Open your mouth and do a short vocaliza-
tion. Listen to the tone and resonance. What is it like now? Rest for a
minute, then stand and see what walking is like.

END OF LESSON

GLASSES

Glasses have a definite and deleterious effect on the voice. There are two reasons for this: pressure and added muscular effort. The weight of glasses is supported by the ears and the bridge of the nose. The pressure on the bridge of the
nose makes it slightly harder to breathe. More important is the effect on the
sinuses. The bridge of the nose is above and adjacent to the sinuses; glasses add
some pressure to the sinuses, compressing them slightly and reducing resonance. The weight of the glasses also means that slightly more effort is necessary to open the mouth and move the jaw. This added effort impedes enunciation slightly. Additionally, glasses require the occipital muscles (the muscles at
the base of the skull and top of the neck) to work harder. If you wear glasses,
you can become aware of this by focusing on the area and removing and putting on your glasses several times. However, do not try this if you feel that you
would obsess about it. Whether this slight tightening affects the voice is

unclear. What is clear is that if you can perform without glasses, you should do so. You will sound better.

OCULAR MUSCLES AND THE SINUSES

The six muscles that move the eyes are located within the eye socket. Four of these muscles are straight, each attaching to one of the four quadrants of the eye. They connect to a common tendon. The other two are oblique, that is, they attach at an angle. One of the oblique muscles attaches to the maxilla. The other five muscles attach to the sphenoid. Both the maxilla and the sphenoid bones have sinuses.

The muscles of the eyelids and brow are also important to visual function. They both control the amount of light into the eye and are responsible for blinking. The muscles of the eyelids are over the sphenoid sinuses, and the muscles of the eyebrows are over the frontal sinus.

When we use our eyes, all these muscle groups—all of them intimately related to the sinus cavities—are involved. Thus excessive tension in the eyes will directly reduce resonance by creating pressure on the sinuses. This effect is in addition to the impact of the eyes on the entire nervous system mentioned earlier. Clearly it is important to keep the eyes soft and relaxed.

The following lesson relates the movement of the eyes to the jaw. Please do the first lesson in this chapter before you attempt this lesson. This will give you a sense of what "soft" eyes are like and facilitate getting maximal benefit from the next lesson.

ATM: EYES RELATE TO JAW

1. Sit in a comfortable chair. **Move your eyes up and down several times.** Notice how smoothly you move your eyes. Did you find the eyes stuttering or jerking several times? **Close your eyes and put your palms over them.** This is called palming. Be sure that you are putting the palms and not the fingers over the eyes. Notice the color before your eyes. When the eyes are relaxed, you will see a velvety black. **Palm your eyes for about a minute. Uncover your eyes and move them up and down again.** Was this any smoother? Pause.

2. **Open and close your mouth.** This is the same as moving your jaw down and up. Repeat this 4 or 5 times. See if you can make the movement softer or gentler each time you do this. Pause.

3. **Move your eyes down as you move your jaw down. Then move your eyes up as you move your jaw up. Move your eyes and jaw up and down several more times.** Does combining these movements make them seem easier or more difficult? **Palm your eyes for a minute.**

4. **Move your eyes up as you move your jaw down. Then go in the other direction. Continue moving your eyes and jaw in opposition 5 or 6 more times. Pause and palm your eyes.** Were you able to keep your eyes comfortable as you moved them in opposition to the jaw?

5. **Move your eyes up and down.** Has this smoothed out any? **Open and close your jaw.** Has it gotten any easier? Can you open your mouth further? Do you notice any other changes? Pause.

This is the end of this module. It is a logical place to stop if you cannot do the lesson in one sitting. Resume at step 6.

---

6. **Move your eyes left and right.** Repeat this several times. Notice how smoothly you make this movement. Do you find it easier going to one side than the other? **Pause. Open your mouth slightly and move your jaw left and right.** Repeat this 4 or 5 times. See if you can make the movement easier each time you do it. Pause, rest for a moment, and palm your eyes.

7. **Move your eyes and jaw to the left and middle.** Repeat this several times. Did you move the jaw and eyes simultaneously? **Now move your eyes left and right twice.** Was there a difference in ease between the two directions? How does this difference, if there is one, relate to the prior movement? **Move your eyes and jaw to the right and back to the middle.** Repeat this several times. Do this with a sense of ease. **Pause. Then move both your eyes and jaw from left to right and back several times.** Pause and palm your eyes for a moment.

8. **Move your eyes to the left as your jaw goes to the right. Return both to the middle and repeat 3 or 4 times.** Which seemed easier, the jaw movement or the eye movement? Or were you unable to tell? Just get a sense of the two; there is no right answer. **Now move your eyes to the right as your jaw goes to the left. Return both to the middle and repeat 3 or 4 times.** Pause. How does your face feel right now? **Move your eyes left and right as your jaw goes right and left.** Repeat this oppositional sequence at least 5 times. Each time see if you can find a way to make it seem easier. Pause and palm your eyes for a minute.

9. **Move your eyes and jaw left and right together.** Do this several times. How has it changed as a result of the movement in opposition? **Move your eyes left and right by themselves.** Has the movement gotten any smoother? **Move your jaw left and right.** Notice whether anything has changed. Pause. **Move your eyes up and down and compare with before. Then move your jaw left and right and look for differences.** Pause and palm your eyes for a minute.

END OF LESSON

12

Pedagogical Uses for This Volume

STUDENT USE

We have deliberately constructed these lessons to adapt to the busy schedule of the performing singer or voice student. Each module lasts about eight to ten minutes and is easily incorporated into the typical ten- to fifteen-minute vocalization/warm-up session that ought to precede any vocal practice. However, all too often, a singer, eager to get to the active part of singing, skips over the most essential part of any rehearsal: body preparation. We hope that these modules will prove so easy, relaxing, and engaging that the singer/student will appreciate the value of the time invested.

GROUP (CLASS) VOICE AND ENSEMBLE REHEARSAL USE

The modular lessons are convenient and easily adapted for use with several students at one time. Again, either as part of the warm-up process or as additional technical information, the teacher can select a lesson that targets a particular area or one that will prepare the entire body for singing. With the teacher reading aloud, students can follow the instructions. Lessons can be assigned to the entire group or to meet the specific needs of an individual.

As with group voice lessons, modules can be incorporated into choral warm-up time as needed. At some point, the choral director might want to give over the bulk of a rehearsal (perhaps just after a concert and before study of new repertoire begins) to guide the entire ensemble through a lesson. We suggest the following strategy, which has achieved amazing results with several choral groups.

1. After the usual vocal warm-ups, have the choir sing a short portion of a work with which they are very familiar.
2. Take the ensemble through the first and second module of any lesson. (Play with this.)
3. Have the ensemble sing the same portion of the same piece. Note any changes in the overall sound and appearance of the group. Solicit changes noted by individual members.
4. Repeat the process by continuing with the next one or two modules in the same lesson.
5. Sing the same portion again and note further changes.

Teacher Use (Private Studio Voice)

Each voice teacher faces a student charged with the following tasks: (1) to assess the vocal production of the student, both pro and con; (2) to diagnose the vocal "faults," or areas that need correction (see McKinney 1994); and (3) to prescribe solutions to correct those areas.

As a voice teacher, Dr. Blades-Zeller has honed her skills of observation and kinesthetic intuition to detect the problematic areas; she has also developed several strategies designed to help the student toward "correction." However, on numerous occasions, having identified areas of tension or "locking up," she felt she needed more than the typical remedial strategies. These Feldenkrais lessons, especially in modular form, provide that extra help.

The modules can be applied as part of the early warm-up/technique-building stage or as "spot fixes" for any particular areas pertinent to the individual student. As a teacher, you can select one module from a lesson and assign it as part of daily practice. Invite the student to explore the modules independently. You can start and stop with module 1, return to that same module the next day, or resume practice with module 2. We invite you to play with them and find out what works for each student and his or her specific needs. In keeping with the Feldenkrais Method's approach and philosophy, there are few "rules" other than that one has to have the patience and desire to listen and respond to what the body communicates.

Appendix

Functional Integration

Functional Integration is one-on-one learning where the practitioner uses gentle touch to guide the student through a lesson. Typically, the student lies on a firm table built expressly for this purpose. Each lesson is crafted for the particular student, although the practitioner may use an Awareness Through Movement lesson as a template. The course of any lesson depends mostly on the student's response to the work and on the practitioner's knowledge and sensitivity, rather than on a predetermined plan. Each lesson has three ingredients: the lesson content, the performance style (or touch), and the organization of the practitioner.

The lesson content of Functional Integration often resembles that of an Awareness Through Movement lesson (ATM) in that it revolves around a function, such as breathing, spinal rotation, or the relationship of the pelvis to the head. However, in Functional Integration the practitioner is free to explore many more diverse options, some of which would not be available to the student without assistance. The peculiarities of the individual can also be taken more into account. Finally, the pacing, range, and variety of options are dictated by the student's response. Thus, even when using the same ATM as the template, the lesson will always look and feel somewhat different for different students. Indeed, at times the lesson that evolves is so radically different from the original plan that a different function is evoked from the one originally expected.

Touch is absolutely critical to the success of a lesson. It must be gentle, noninvasive, and directionally clear. A harsh touch will tighten the student's system, creating resistance to the lesson content. The touch must not invade the person's sense of self or it will be rejected. Thus, if an area "doesn't want to move," that must be respected. This noninvasiveness allows the nervous system to accept the lesson as its own rather than as something that has been imposed on it.

Finally, the directions must be clear; otherwise, instead of a lesson, the session becomes an unintelligible series of sensations.

When two organisms are linked by touch, they become in a real sense one interconnected system. Thus, the student is constantly aware of the practitioner's organization, even if this awareness is unconscious. The practitioner is also constantly aware of the student's organization. Much of this awareness is at levels below conceptual consciousness. Hence, at times the practitioner is able to infer the student's needs without quite knowing how or why. As a result of this interconnection, there is an implicit information flow from the better to the less organized system. In most cases this is from practitioner to student. Thus, there can be improvement in the student's functioning that is, to some extent, separate from the content of the lesson.

A successful lesson results in the student's integrating the desired changes—more mobility, less pain, or the ability to perform a given task better—into daily life. Some successful lessons may not be immediately realized by the student. It may take several days to process fully the information received and feel the changes.

Glossary

actuate. To move to action.

adductors. Muscles whose contraction effects a drawing together or closure toward a median axis (as in a coming together of the vocal folds [cords] during phonation).

Awareness Through Movement lessons. Group lessons where students are verbally guided through movement sequences by a practitioner.

carpal tunnel syndrome. A common form of repetitive-stress injury. It involves pain, weakness, and numbness in the hand and wrist. Usually blamed on a pressure on the median nerve in the space formed by the wrist cones and carpal ligaments.

diaphragm. The partition of muscles and tendons between the thoracic (chest) cavity and the abdominal cavity. Functions as a partition between the two regions and is an important muscle for respiration.

Functional Integration. A one-to-one learning process, where the movements are communicated through slow, gentle touch. The practitioner guides the student through a series of precise movements that alter habitual patterns and provide new learning directly to the neuromuscular system.

heuristic. Stimulating interest or investigation.

hyoid bone. The U-shaped bone at the base of the tongue to which the larynx connects and from which it is suspended by ligaments.

intercostal muscles. Short external and internal muscles between the ribs.

kinesiology. The study of the mechanics of human movement.

kinesthetic awareness. The ability to feel and monitor changes in the levels of tension and movement of the muscles and joints.

larynx. The structure of muscle and cartilage positioned at the top of the trachea and containing the vocal folds; the "voice box."

lordosis. An excessive forward curve in the lower spine. Also known as swayback.

module. A distinct section of a larger piece of work, body, or structure.

palate. The roof of the mouth (buccal cavity). Consists of the alveolar ridge and the hard and soft palate.

pedagogy. The science and art of teaching.

pharynx. The throat wall, specifically from the velum down to the larynx.

proprioception. The sense that is concerned with knowing the position of a body part without having to see it.

registration (register). "A series of consecutive tones of equal (or similar) timbre, which can be distinguished from adjoining series of tones" (Miller 1986, 312).

sacroiliac. A fibrous joint, the part of the pelvic girdle between the sacrum and the iliac (see illustration, p. 57). There are two, one on each side.

sacrum. Five fused vertebrae that form a solid bone directly below the lumbar spine (lower back) and above the coccyx (tailbone). The sacrum forms part of the pelvic girdle.

sternum. The breastbone, a thin, flat structure of bone and cartilage to which most of the ribs (except the bottom two pairs of "floating ribs") are attached at the front of the chest.

thoracic cavity. The chest cavity, containing the heart, lungs, part of the trachea, and the esophagus.

tone. Normal tension or responsiveness to stimuli; specifically, muscular tonus.

tonus. A state of partial contraction characteristic of normal muscle.

uvula. Pendular muscle at the posterior of the velum; it hangs like a sac.

velum. The soft palate, that is, the soft posterior portion of the roof of the mouth.

vestibular system. Structure located in the inner ear that helps the body maintain balance and orientation by monitoring the sensations of movement and position.

References and Resources

REFERENCES

Alderson, Richard. 1979. *The Complete Book of Voice Training.* West Nyack, N.Y.: Parker.

Bunch, Meribeth. 1995. *Dynamics of the Singing Voice.* Vienna: Springer-Verlag.

Christy, Van. 1967. *Expressive Singing.* New York: McGraw Hill.

Coffin, Berton. 1989. *Historical Vocal Pedagogy Classics.* Metuchen, N.J.: Scarecrow Press.

Feldenkrais, Moshe. 1949. *Body and Mature Behavior: A Study of Anxiety, Sex, Gravitation, and Learning.* New York: International Universities Press.

———. 1985. *The Potent Self.* Ed. Michaeleen Kimmey. San Francisco: Harper & Row.

Garcia, Manuel. *Exercises and Method for Singing.* In *Historical Vocal Pedagogy Classics,* ed. Berton Coffin. Metuchen, N.J.: Scarecrow Press, 1989.

Gorman, David. 1983. *The Body Moveable.* Guelph, Ont.: Ampersand.

Henderson, Larra Browning. 1979. *How to Train Singers.* West Nyack, N.Y.: Parker.

McKinney, James, ed. 1994. *Diagnosis and Correction of Vocal Faults.* Nashville, Tenn.: Genevox Music.

Miller, Richard. 1986. *The Structure of Singing: System and Art of Vocal Technique.* New York: Schirmer Books.

Nair, Garyth. 1999. *Voice: Tradition and Technology: A State-of-the-Art-Studio.* San Diego: Singular.

Norretranders, Tor. 1998. *The User Illusion: Cutting Consciousness Down to Size.* New York: Viking.

Schmidt, Jan. 1998. *Basics of Singing.* New York: Schirmer Books.

Shafarman, Steven. 1997. *Awareness Heals: The Feldenkrais Method for Dynamic Health.* Reading, Mass.: Addison-Wesley.

Spence, Alexander P., and Elliot B. Mason. 1992. *Human Anatomy and Physiology.* Saint Paul, Minn: West.

Todd, Mabel Ellswort. [1937] 1968. *The Thinking Body.* Princeton, N.J.: Princeton Book.

Travell, Janet M., and David G. Simons. 1983. *Myofascial Pain and Dysfunction: The Trigger Point Manual.* Baltimore: Williams & Wilkins.

Vennard, William. 1967. *Singing: The Mechanism and the Technique.* New York: Carl Fischer.

Ware, Clifton. 1998. *Basics of Vocal Pedagogy.* New York: McGraw Hill.

RESOURCES

Alon, Ruthy. 1990. *Mindful Spontaneity: Moving in Tune with Nature*. Dorset, England: Prism. (Available in the United States through Avery Publishing Group, New York.)

Feldenkrais, Moshe. 1972, 1977, *Awareness Through Movement*. New York: Harper & Row.

————. 1977. *The Case of Nora: Body Awareness as Healing*. New York: Harper & Row.

————. 1981. *The Elusive Obvious*. Cupertino, Calif.: Meta Publications.

————. 1984. *The Master Moves*. Cupertino, Calif.: Meta Publications.

Rywerant, Yochanan. 1983. *The Feldenkrais Method: Teaching by Handling*. San Francisco: Harper & Row.

Zemach-Bersin, David, Kaethe Zemach-Bersin, and Mark Reese. 1990. *Relaxercise: The Easy New Way to Health and Fitness*. San Francisco: Harper & Row.

Feldenkrais Guild of North America, 1-800-775-2118.

Visit the Feldenkrais Web site, www.feldenkrais.com, for information on practitioners on all six inhabited continents.

Index of Lessons

AREAS OF INTEREST AND CORRESPONDING LESSONS

Lessons that are most useful for a particular concern are listed in order of likely usefulness.

General Index

About the Authors

SAMUEL H. NELSON is a graduate of the Toronto Professional Feldenkrais Training Program (1987). He has offered Awareness Through Movement classes to the public since 1985. He has held a seminar on the Feldenkrais Method each semester at the Eastman School of Music for the past thirteen years and has presented seminars at music schools in Indiana and Ohio. He has also presented workshops for musicians at several area high schools, as well as for physical therapists and equestrians. He has a private practice in Rochester, New York. He is the author of "Playing with the Entire Self: The Feldenkrais Method and Musicians" (*Seminars in Neurology,* June 1989). He holds a B.A. and an M.A. in economics; his Ph.D. in environmental sciences is from the University of Wisconsin, Madison. Before becoming a Feldenkrais Practitioner, he worked in the Energy and Environmental Systems Division at Argonne National Laboratory.

ELIZABETH BLADES-ZELLER holds both doctor of musical arts and master's degrees from the Eastman School of Music, where she received the 1990 Eastman Graduate Teaching Assistant Award for Excellence in Teaching. As a graduate assistant at Eastman, she participated in the development of a new syllabus for the vocal pedagogy course. At the request of the music education department, she redesigned and wrote the syllabi for the two-semester voice methods class. She is a Phi Beta Kappa, magna cum laude graduate of Skidmore College and also received a master of science degree from the University of Kansas. She is associate professor of voice, coordinator of the voice area, and director of opera at Heidelberg College in Tiffin, Ohio, where she teaches applied voice, vocal pedagogy, and language diction. She is engaged in qualitative research in vocal pedagogy; her forthcoming book, *A Spectrum of Voices* (Scarecrow Press), is based on her ongoing study of exemplary voice teaching.